CRYSTAL GAZING

Jabberwoke Pocket Occult Collection

~

Crystal Gazing by Frater Achad

Heavenly Bridegrooms by Ida Craddock

Moonchild by Aleister Crowley

The Kybalion by Three Initiates

The So-Called Occult by Carl Jung

The Great God Pan by Arthur Machen

The Witch Cult by Margaret Murray

The Book of Lies by Frater Perdurabo

A Midsommar Night's Dream by William Shakespeare

Satan: A Novel by Mark Twain

~

CRYSTAL VISION THROUGH CRYSTAL GAZING

OR
THE CYSTAL AS A STEPPING
STONE TO CLEAR VISION

A PRACTICAL TREASTIE ON THE REAL
VALUE OF CRYSTAL GAZING

BY
FRATER ACHAD

Author of
"Q.B.L. or THE BRIDE'S RECEPTION"
and "THE CHALICE OF ECSTASY."

JABBERWOKE
San Francisco

CRYSTAL GAZING Copyright © 1917 Frater Achad

POCKET OCCULT EDITION Copyright © 2021 by Jabberwo[ke]

All rights reserved.

Printed in the USA.

First Jabberwoke Paperback Edition: February 2021.

Designed by S.R.L.

Cover Art by Summer Candy

This edition has been edited for formatting and content.

Paperback ISBN: 978-1-954873-36-0

Library of Congress Control Number: 2021942213

10 9 8 7 6 5 4 3 2 1

FraterAchadCrystalGazing.com

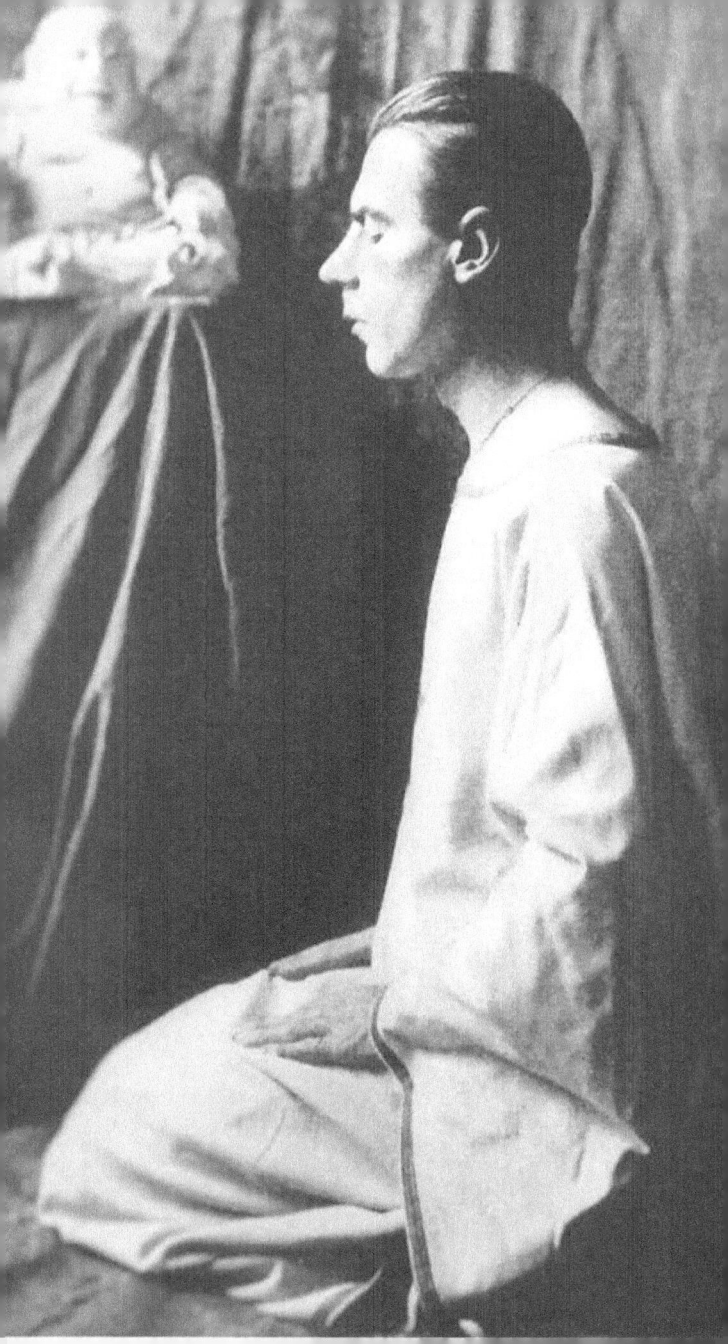

Foreword

THE PURPOSE of this little volume is threefold. (1) To give those who are interested in the art of Crystal-Gazing a clear and concise method of procedure, not alone in the practice of the work, but also in the preparation of the crystal itself, so that it becomes a true material basis or link with other planes. (2) To show that the Ancient Methods of Working – if properly understood – are more scientific than modern ones, since they were designed to insure a definite type of vision and to put the Seer in touch with definite Intelligences of a Higher Order. (3) To point out that there are other Crystalline Spheres besides the crystal ball at first used to contact them; and that eventually the practice may lead to very high results, if the necessary steps are taken to insure success.

With these objects in mind, the Author has done all in his power to make this book of real value to all who may obtain it. In the hands of the beginner it may lead to a wider conception of the Nature and Powers of his, or her, own being. Those who have already traveled some distance along the Occult Path may still find help through the study of the more advanced, if less understood, methods of the Ancient Seers. Those who are seeking to make their own Vision more Perfect, so that the Light of Truth may focus itself within them, will also find hints as to the means of accomplishing their True Purpose.

Thus, it is hoped, all will be satisfied; and should their satisfaction be equal to that of the Author at this opportunity to herald the Light – however faintly – of the Ultimate Crystalline Sphere, Whose nature is Light Itself, he will be more than repaid for his efforts.

FRATER ACHAD.

Contents

I	The Lesser Crystalline Sphere	1
II.	The Greater Crystalline Sphere	15
III.	The Universal Crystalline Sphere	31
IV.	A Consideration of Ancient Methods	45
V.	Further Considerations	63
VI.	The Attainment of Crystal Vision	75
VII.	Of the Ultimate Crystal	89
	Afterwards: *A Master of the Temple*	101

CYRSTAL GAZING

I

The Lesser Crystalline Sphere

THE study of crystal gazing without a Crystal would appear very much like the study of a "Bill of Fare" without troubling to obtain the material food described thereon. The mere reading of a book on a subject of this nature without an attempt to put into practice the processes described – step by step – from the very beginning, is futile and a mere waste of time.

The first consideration, therefore (if the would-be seer has not already attended to the matter), will be the choice of a suitable Crystal to form the material basis of his experiments and a stepping-stone to the development of his latent powers of clear vision.

In all probability the aspirant to this ancient art has already been attracted to a Crystal Sphere of this nature, for there is little doubt of the extraordinary magnetic attracttion of objects of this kind whenever they are exposed to our view, and since the present interest in this fascinating subject has become apparent, we may see these Crystals displayed more publicly than has ever been the case in the past.

FRATER ACHAD

In olden times, and even up to the last few years, crystals were the cherished possessions of those well advanced upon the Path and kept by them from the eyes of the so-called profane. Only after having found the way, often with difficulty, to the presence of these Seers, did an opportunity occur to get even a glimpse of such a magical link with the invisible spheres. Fortunately for the modern aspirant, however, this difficulty has been removed and it has been found that more good may result by a proper study of this science so as to develop one's own latent powers, than ever a mere visit to a Seer could produce. Man has made a considerable advance on the road to Attainment. Self-development and self-initiation are beginning to play a much more prominent part than formerly. Man is no longer content to believe what he is told, he at last desires to *know* from his own experience. The Crystal is a stepping-stone towards Self-knowledge.

We should select our crystal with great care; the more perfect its quality, the more we should desire it as the means of our development. It should be neither too large, nor too small, and here our natural intuition should be allowed to guide us, but I may say that it is not well that the Sphere be less than two and one-half inches in diameter, and it is not necessary that it be more than four. We should choose

CRYSTAL GAZING

this crystal, I might almost say, lovingly; at least, if a selection is presented to us we should take the one to which, after a moment of silent consideration, we feel most attracted; and this – if possible – regardless of the material consideration of its cost. We should not, however, purchase a globe which is far beyond our material means, so that other obligations would suffer thereby; otherwise, lurking at the back of our consciousness whenever we use it, may be the feeling of having acted wrongly in that connection from the very start.

We must realize the importance of this advice, for the great attraction that the Crystal has for us is something more than the arousing of a mere idle curiosity on our part. It is no less than a desire – subconscious it may be – to attain the same purity of soul that we perceive in the Crystal before us, and, as a matter of fact the results we obtain by a study and practice of this Art will largely, if not entirely, depend on the purity of our desire and the quality and state of development of our inner nature.

That is why I am taking up the material consideration first of all, for after the crystal has actually come into our possession, our path lies away from such considerations, at least until we have attained the success which will surely attend our earnest efforts in the right direction.

Let us suppose then that the first step has been taken, a suitable Crystal has been obtained, and that the possessor has taken it into his own room – the one he likes best and wherein he feels most contented and serene. The choice of this room is also of importance, though in this case we must make the best of what is at our disposal. If possible this room should be one wherein we have never had any particularly unpleasant experience, where there is nothing that we feel antipathy towards, and wherein are such objects as we love best of all our possessions. In such an atmosphere the soul of the seer will feel at peace, free from distractions, and consequently in the right mood to commence his studies.

The Crystal should first be taken in both hands and held for a few moments while we close our eyes and, calming the mind, raise our consciousness to the highest and purest Ideal of which we are capable. We should persist in our effort toward this state until we *feel* that holy calm and stillness, so well symbolized by the Crystal itself.

We should next turn our attention to the crystal, separating the thumbs slightly, thus allowing it to rest easily in the hollow of our hands. We should remember that we, too, rest

CRYSTAL GAZING

thus in the Hollow of the Hand of the Almighty without Whose aid, our Work must come to naught.

As we look into the depths of this Globe – material though it be – we cannot but be impressed with ideas of Purity. It is almost as if we gazed into the eyes of a little child, and there are few who have not experienced a peculiar sensation, almost amounting to awe, certainly one of wonder, when so doing. The soul of the seer is very like that of a little child – or should be – and it is in order that we may regain the purity and perfection of this childlike vision that we set out on this path. Most of our material surroundings give us a certain feeling of grossness, few, if any, can compare with the lucid depths of the crystal now before us.

But, in entering this path, we are about to deal with ideas and forces, finer and less apparent to our ordinary senses than any we have yet known. Even the transparent crystal is not as yet entirely pure, though we may be unable to perceive one spot on its surface or within its depths.

It is charged with a certain subtle magnetism attracted to it from the surroundings in which it has been prior to the time we obtained it. It has passed through many hands before, for a few moments, it rested in our own while we turned our thoughts inward and upward towards the Highest. Even as our own aspiration at that moment was pure, so must we first purify this symbol of our Inner-self – the Diamond Soul as it is sometimes called – for purification is the **first** step in the process whereby Initiation may be obtained. We must pass this material thing – inorganic and lifeless though it may seem to us – through the same processes of Purification, Consecration and Initiation, through which we in turn desire to pass.

But how may this be accomplished? That is not so difficult as it might at first appear, but it is quite necessary for all that, and in order to impress this necessity on your minds I must first devote a little time to an explanation of the process.

Every material object, including the physical body of man himself, is but the outward expression of certain finer forms of matter which interpenetrate it. Thus in the case of man, we may say he is composed of body, soul and spirit, the soul, in that case, being the plastic medium which enables the Pure Essence or Spirit to contact and communicate with the outer physical shell or envelope. This Soul of man – and of the World – is sometimes called "The Astral Light" or "Plastic Mediator", for unlike grosser sub-stances it may be readily molded at will and without visible means. This Astral Light interpenetrates all

CRYSTAL GAZING

objects, it is invisible to our physical senses, but its existence both in man and in all nature, makes possible the power of Clairvoyance – Clear Vision – as well as of Clairaudience and other powers the develop-ment of which does not come within the scope of the present treatise.

This subtle magnetic fluid is everywhere present, and reflected upon it – as in a mirror – may be found all the events or pictures of what has occurred, or what is occurring on this planet and even beyond this sphere. The Astral light absorbs every least impression, and so, even though not apparent to our normal and undeveloped senses, the astral counterpart of our Crystal Globe is still charged with impressions of all kinds that have accumulated within it since its material substance was first formed. It is because of its attracting these subtle influences that we wish to make use of it as a medium for bringing them to our own consciousness, but we must in the first instance demagnetize it, so as to banish all trace of the past influences which it still contains.

This may be simply accomplished as follows:

Purification

First place the crystal on a slender cup-like stand. (One may usually be obtained with the crystal in the first instance.) This stand should be placed on the surface of a small table, which has previously been carefully cleansed, and from which all other objects have been removed.

We may either stand or sit before this table, within easy reach of the *crystal* while we perform the first step towards the purification of our *material basis*. Next place the tips of the fingers of both hands together, the thumbs being also joined, so as to form a circle – symbol of infinity but also of a limitation or boundary – then *concentrate the attention* on this circle until you clearly imagine, or actually feel, a film *of fine astral matter*, like the film of a soap-bubble, formed of the fine substance of your own astral and etheric bodies, spreading over the hollow space between your hands. As in the former instance, when your whole attention was turned within, this film should represent to you the highest and purest of which you are capable. A film of such purity that it will have the effect of dispelling or banishing every lower influence it contacts.

Having concentrated your mind in this way for a few moments – and the ease with which this is accomplished is a good test of your powers as a crystal-gazer – you must now slowly move your hands until they are directly above the crystal on the table, and still keeping your mind firmly fixed on the idea of this pure film of astral matter, pass your *hands*

CRYSTAL GAZING

down over the crystal, thus causing it, in its turn, to pass clear through the magnetized circle of your hands.

When your hands reach the table at the base of the stand, they should be drawn apart, thus breaking the "film" and leaving the crystal above demagnetized of all that is of a lower vibration than your own highest ideal. It is then like a blank talisman, or a thing without life. If this first step has been successfully accomplished, the crystal will now give an impression of perfect 'cleanliness,' or that is the best description one can give of the proper result obtained by the process of purification. It must on no account be touched at this stage of the work.

The next process is to charge it with your own magnetism, thus *consecrating* it to the Work you wish to accomplish.

Consecration

If the best results are to be obtained the crystal must now be *consecrated* or dedicated to the special mission for which it is destined. This mission is a very important one, much greater than we at first imagined perhaps, for it is no less than that of *representing to the seer his own Soul in the pure condition to which he aspires to bring it.* For that reason, his material basis, the crystal, must never be used for any but the highest purposes. It is no longer an ornament that may be placed on the mantel-shelf, but something he is about to endow with his own life, to charge with his own highest Will. Thus it becomes something most sacred to him, no longer an object to be idly handled by the profane any more than he would allow his own innermost feelings and ideals to be thus roughly used by every passing stranger. This explains the attitude of the true Seer of the past; it is not so much that the Crystals they used became objects of superstitious mystery to the ignorant, as this sacred value to the Seer himself, which caused them to be so carefully preserved. Once we understand this, we shall adopt the right attitude towards our studies from the very start.

How then must we accomplish the Consecration of our Small Crystalline Sphere?

Leaving it just where it stands on the table before us we must next place the tips of our fingers and thumbs together, very much as before, but this time allowing them to form a perfect equilateral *triangle*. Our hands should be held in this position over the crystal, while we strongly *concentrate our minds* on the idea that *a positive current* is flowing from them down into the crystal. This current must again represent our highest aspiration in its purest form, but directed this time by our True Will. When we fairly feel this current flowing from our hands, they should be passed gently over

CRYSTAL GAZING

the crystal – still forming the triangle as before but gradually allowing the palms to encircle the globe, without actually touching it; then, when we feel impressed to do so as by an unseen force, we should gently but firmly grasp the crystal itself, lifting it from its stand, and allowing our hands to pass all over its surface. All this while the mind must be kept in the highest possible condition of pure aspiration, as if we were giving our very life to this object, as indeed we are, for it now becomes more than a mere symbol of dead matter, it lives, and we have brought it to birth as a child of our Will. Henceforth it must be treated as such, as a sacred instrument, dedicated and consecrated to the service of the Highest.

And here a warning is necessary, though it will not be needed by the aspirant to this Art who has followed the directions hitherto given in the right spirit. This warning was also given by an earlier writer on this subject, John Melville, he writes:

"A sure and certain law exists, viz: - That if the seer's *purpose* be *evil* when he or she uses the crystal or mirror, it will *react* upon the seer sooner or later *with terrible effect;* wherefore all are strictly cautioned to *be good* and *do good* only."

This may sound rather like Sunday-school talk, but when explained in the light of the principles I have set forth above, it becomes clear, for we thereby charge the body of our "child" – the crystal – with a force which must inevitably return to us as its creator, quite apart from any question of outside influence from "beings" on other planes.

But he again reminds us that "The aerial spaces are *thronged* with countless intelligence – celestial, *good, pure, true,* and the *reverse.* The latter have *force:* the former possess *power.* To reach the good ones, *the heart of the gazer must correspond,* and they should be invoked with prayerful feelings.

There are innumerable multitudes of the *bad* on the confines of Matter and - Spirt. These malign forces are many and terrible; but they can never reach the soul that relies on God in perfect faith, and which only Invokes the Good, the Beautiful, and True for noble purposes."

Here we have many fresh ideas that need to be dealt with more fully in their proper place, but the advice is good, and the warning necessary to those who, with the best intentions, may through ignorance of their own nature, and that of the Universe in which they live and move and have their being, imprudently attract to themselves forces of evil too great for them to withstand, thus bringing about obsession, madness or even worse, through use of wrong methods.

CRYSTAL GAZING

Initiation

This stage in the process of the preparation of our crystal has been partially accomplished in the previous section of the work. We have really *Consecrated* the object by determining to use it only for the one work before us and for no other purpose, and we have at least partially *Initiated* it by charging it with our own Will and Life. Initiation means a beginning and we shall have made a good beginning If the above instructions have been carefully and faithfully followed. An elaborate ceremony might have been adopted, but since we are ourselves only making a beginning of the Work, such a Ceremony, even if described would have appeared cumbersome and unwieldy. As it is the merest novice has no excuse for neglecting the few simple rules laid down, which in the end, will be seen to have a far greater importance than is at first imagined.

If we start rightly we shall continue rightly, but a false start practically ruins our chances of success.

Enough has been accomplished for the moment, and the next step is to leave the crystal *alone* for a short time, not to start to use it immediately. This will be a test of patience, for one thing, and we shall need all our patience in order to succeed fully.

FRATER ACHAD

But, as with a new born babe, we must not leave our crystal unprotected. It should be carefully wrapped in a piece of silk obtained for the purpose and likewise dedicated to that end. Rose-pink is perhaps the best, as if to suggest our pure love of this "object" we have so carefully prepared. Outside that we might well place "grey" and finally "black" silk wrappings.

If this seems too elaborate, use a piece of pure black silk only, and whenever the Little Crystalline Sphere is used, first polish it carefully with this same silk wrapper.

Now put your crystal away, and read the next Chapter carefully before attempting to use it further.

II

The Greater Crystalline Sphere

WE have given some consideration to the proper preparation of our Crystal, or, as we termed it in the last chapter, the Lesser Crystalline Sphere. We must now pay some attention to the necessary condition of our own Inner Being or what we may term The Greater Crystalline Sphere.

The attitude of mind in which we approach the practice of the Art of Crystal-Gazing, will largely determine the results to be obtained therefrom. These may be little or great, as we ourselves look at the matter from a narrow or broad point of view.

Those who enter upon this study, actuated by a mere idle curiosity, after having attempted to satisfy it, may find there is apparently very little to be gained, while, on the other hand, even if in the first instance curiosity alone was our motive, it may give place to a genuine and lasting interest, leading to the highest results, if we are prepared to add to our original impulse enough energy to carry us through the very necessary preliminary practices by which alone, success may be assured.

There are two important factors entering into this proposition, The Seer or Gazer and the Crystal or object used to concentrate the gaze upon. The proper relation of these two is what brings about the desired result, viz: Clear Vision.

Now the clarity of our vision depends chiefly upon ourselves, not upon the crystal which is but a convenient means of acquiring this. We should now spend a few minutes in self-examination, in the same way that we did when we first examined the crystal or material basis of the work.

Why have we been attracted to the crystal. is just as important a question as why did the crystal attract us? In fact much more important, for our whole future may depend upon this curious meeting. Was it because we had been told, or that we imagined, that by some mysterious means we should thereby be enabled to peer into the future there to discover what lies before us on Life's Path, or what lies before those whom we hold dear as friends or acquaintances? Was it that we might perchance see the vision of one whom we had idealized in our imagination as a soulmate, and hoped thereby to be assured of the actual existence of such? Was it that we might pry into the distant past, or even into the immediate past, of the lives of those with whom we are in daily contact, so that we might

CRYSTAL GAZING

thereby obtain a knowledge of events that would at the same time put us in possession of a certain degree of power? Or was it as a stepping stone to really Clear Vision, a better understanding of Life itself, of our own being, and our true relationship with our environment in a larger sense than could be expected by mere physical means?

Probably our motives may have been compounded of some or all of these, and many more, and on that account be somewhat vague and uncertain. In that case we must at first expect a certain vagueness and uncertainty in our visions. In proportion to the clarity of our own conceptions, must our visions appear hazy or perfect in every way. "A true vision is to awakement as awakement is to a dream: and a perfect vision is so nearly perfect Reality that words cannot be found in which to translate it, yet it must not be forgotten that its truth ceases on return of the seer to the Material plane". This statement was made by one of the Great Seers, one who no longer needs the aid of a crystal, yet it holds good in this case also and will give the aspirant a glimpse of what may be expected provided we go to the trouble to thus perfect our instrument – the Greater Crystalline Sphere.

A certain honesty of purpose is requisite to this Art, that is to say if it is our true desire to obtain the beat results. The Good the Beautiful and the True are the natural desires of the human soul, any inclination towards the reverse, shows an imperfection in our Crystalline Sphere which needs to be eradicated. Fortunately the Soul of man is Plastic and unlike the Hard Crystal Globe, may be easily worked upon and remolded nearer to the heart's desire.

A certain honesty of purpose must also be apparent in the instructions we follow, and for that reason it may be well to say a few words about the "crystals" and books on Crystal-Gazing which may come into the hands of the Student.

First then in regard to Crystals and "crystals". In all probability the crystal you have purchased, purified, consecrated, initiated and wrapped away so carefully, is not a real crystal at all. This news may come to you with a kind of sickening shock. But this shock will not last long if your own "Greater Crystal" the Inner Part of your being is true, and if you have faithfully carried out the preliminary instructions as directed. You have accepted this symbolic crystal as your "child", as something into which you have directed your highest aspiration and will. It matters little what the substance is composed of, so long as it has now become for you a sacred thing.

But how could you have been thus deceived if such were the case. Through ignorance of the real value of Crystal. In all probability the ball you purchased cost but a few dollars, whereas, had it been genuine Crystal, it would have been much beyond your means, or at least have cost more than you were prepared to risk on the experiment in hand. You have probably obtained a very carefully cut and polished sphere of glass, free from flaws and difficult and expensive to make. But it is a manufactured article, not a natural stone. It may be you could see little difference between it and a genuine stone, but the difference lies *within,* for the real crystal is built up by Nature on hexagonal lines, yet so clear and transparent is the stone that we do not see them. The one true test of all the crystal family is the fact that the *angle of incidence* remains the same in each species. Now the Hexagram symbolizes the Macrocosm, the Great Universe, or God. For the moment we have described the Soul of Man as our Greater Crystalline Sphere. In many cases this Soul has not attained to its greatest purity, and is little more than the Glass Sphere is to the Genuine Crystal.

Let this teach you your first great lesson in the Art, not to be deceived by, appearances, for it is written "The Devil himself may appear to us as an Angel of Light". Yet do not be discouraged by this discovery, let us examine the matter more closely. Crystals are comparatively rare, and while little in demand, and that only by the most earnest seekers and Seers who were prepared to "Buy their eggs without haggling", the supply was ample to fill the needs of those who sought after them. Today Crystal-Gazing has taken a more popular aspect, and attracts – in many instances – less serious people, or those who are not prepared to pay very highly for the fulfillment of their desires. Consequently a demand has arisen for "something very like the real" – just as good perhaps for the majority of persons – but, what is more serious, there is likely to be a corresponding decline in the value of the practice, for less care may be taken in the methods used, and so on, till – like many other studies – it fails to be understood and thus falls into disrepute.

Fortunately the matter is not irreparable when understood in its true light, and greater reliance placed upon the inner powers of the Seer than on the objects at which he gazes. He cannot change glass into crystal in the case of the globe before him, but he may change Glass into Crystal in the case of his own Inner Being, and the latter is far the most important consideration after all.

Next, in regard to books on the subject of Crystal-Gazing, we find the Art mentioned here and there in a great many Ancient and Modern treatises on Occult matters, but there

CRYSTAL GAZING

are few books of a serious nature devoted entirely to this subject. What we do see are usually produced in such a catch-penny style that they are immediately associated with 'fortune-telling' and 'dream-books' of the lowest order.

There is one little book, however, that is well worthy of notice as it is evidently an earnest effort on the part of the Author to set forth the main principles, as far as known to him, in a truly helpful manner. I refer to "Crystal Gazing and Clairvoyance" by John Melville. Published London 1910 by Nichols and Co. in a new and revised form. I shall refer to this little book again from time to time, First the composition of Beryls or Crystals is taken up; but for reasons mentioned earlier in this chapter, this aspect is of no great importance to the modern enquirer. Then the derivation of the name is discussed and certain other matters of a hypothetical nature are enquired into. The Ancient Methods of Ceremonial in connection with the Art are summarized, and a few practical directions for the modern student follow. This concludes the first part of the book dealing particularly with the matter in hand. The second part is by another author, and entitled "Hygienic Clairvoyance", the title being a most un-fortunate one in my opinion, although there are some interesting hints in regard to "Induced

Clairvoyance" towards the end of the book. But there is no *connected* and systematic thread to guide the student through the various stages that may be necessary for him in order to attain a complete knowledge and experience of the whole matter. For that reason, having been requested to prepare a new and original account of the processes involved, I have decided to start at the very beginning, and lead the student by gradual stages to a comprehension of the larger outcome of the Work.

But it is now time for us to consider the early stages of the practical work, taking up the thread from where we left it at the end of the last chapter.

Therefore take your crystal and polish it carefully placing it upon its stand near you, while you pay attention to the following directions.

In the first instance your desire is merely to cultivate a certain degree of clairvoyant power by the regular use of this globe. By this means what are called "visions" of things or events, past, present or future may appear clearly to the inner sight or eye of the soul.

No great harm can come from this practice, provided that the inner motives of the Seer are kept pure and no attempt is made to prostitute it to undesirable ends. Looked upon as a process of self-development leading to

CRYSTAL GAZING

concentration of the powers of the mind, and a widening of the mental horizon, the practice of this art may be recommended to almost everyone.

The rules laid down by John Melville for this stage of the work are clear and concise, and leave little to be desired, I shall therefore quote them practically in full, adding my own comments, where necessary, in parentheses.

(1) "Select a quiet room where you will be entirely undisturbed, taking care that it is as far as possible free from mirrors, ornaments, pictures, glaring colors and the like, which may otherwise distract the attention.

"This room should be of a comfortable temperature in accordance with the time of year, neither too hot nor too cold. About 60° to 65° Fahr. is suitable in most cases, though allowance can be made for natural differences in the temperaments of various persons. Thus thin, nervous, delicately organized in-dividuals, and those of lymphatic and soft, easy-going, passive types, require a slightly warmer apartment than the more positive class, who are known by their *dark* eyes, hair and complexion, combined with more prominent joints and sharper development of what phrenologists term the Perceptive region of the forehead. Should a fire, or any form of artificial light be necessary, it should be well screened off, so as to prevent the light rays from being reflected in, or in any manner directly reaching the crystal.

"The room should not be dark, but rather shadowed, or charged with dull light, some-what such as prevails on a cloudy or wet day.

(2) "The crystal should be placed on its stand on a table, or it may rest on a black velvet cushion, but in either case it should be partially surrounded by a black silk or similar wrap or screen, so adjusted as to cut off any undesirable reflection.

"Before beginning to experiment, remember that most frequently nothing will be seen on the first occasion, and possibly not for several sittings, though some sitters, if strongly gifted with psychic powers in a state of unconscious, and sometimes conscious degree of unfoldment, may be fortunate enough to obtain good results at the very first trial.

"If, therefore, nothing is perceived during the first few attempts, do not despair or become impatient or imagine that you will never see anything.

"There is a royal road to crystal vision, but it is open only to the compound password of Calmness, Patience, Perseverance. If at the first attempt to ride a bicycle failure ensues, the only way to learn is to pay attention to the

CRYSTAL GAZING

necessary rules, and to *persevere daily* until the ability to ride comes naturally.

"Thus it is with the would-be seer. Persevere in accordance with these simple directions, and success will sooner or later crown your efforts.

(3) "Commence by sitting comfortably with the eyes fixed upon the crystal, not by a fierce stare, but with a steady, calm gaze, for ten minutes only, on the first occasion. In taking the time it is best to hang your watch at a distance where, while the face is clearly visible, the ticking is rendered inaudible. When the time is up, carefully put the crystal away in its case, and keep it in a dark place, under lock and key, allowing no one but yourself to handle it."

(The importance of this latter in-struction will be clear to those who have studied the first chapter of this present treatise, and who have actually prepared their crystals in the proper manner. Strange magnetism will of course have its effect on the crystal globe, and again render necessary some such process of Purification as already described.)

"At the second sitting, which should be at the same place, in the same position, and at the same time, you may increase the length of the effort to fifteen minutes, and continue for this period during the next five or six sittings, after

25

which the time may be *gradually* increased, but should in no case exceed one hour."

(The first instruction in the above paragraph, relative to place, time, etc., is given in order that the student may take advantage of certain Cyclic Laws, which make the repetition of an act under similar circumstances, easier with each attempt, on account of the fact that he has begun to *form a habit* of working.)

(4) "Any person, or persons admitted to the room, and allowed to remain while you sit should (a) keep absolute silence and (b) remain seated at a distance from you."

(The presence of any other person is of course a handicap to concentration of mind, and should be avoided at first. Any movement in the room may reflect in the crystal, and thus disturb the vision.)

"When you have developed your latent powers, questions may, of course, be put to you by one of those present, but even then only in a very gentle, or low and slow tone of voice; never suddenly, or in a forceful manner."

(It is far better to make the whole practice one of self-development, and not to have people around who will ask a lot of idle questions. Again, the soul of the seer is to some extent thrown open during the practice, so as to make impressions from the Higher Spheres possible, and it is quite another matter to let other, probably

CRYSTAL GAZING

ignorant, people, pump the mind of the seer full of suggestions of a lower order, while in that condition. Therein lies the danger of the practice.)

(5) "When you find the crystal begins to look dull or cloudy, with small pin points of light glittering therein, like tiny stars, you may know that you are *commencing* to obtain that for which you seek - viz: crystalline vision. Therefore persevere with confidence. This condition may, or may not, continue for several sittings, the crystal seeming at times to alternately appear and disappear as in a mist. By and by this hazy appearance will in its turn give place quite suddenly to a blindness of the senses to all else but a blue or bluish ocean of space, against which, as if it were a background, *the vision* will be clearly apparent."

(The above is practically all the instruction necessary to the desired result, the rest is *practice* on your part. Yet here are a few further hints for your guidance:)

(6) "The crystal should not be used soon after taking a meal, and care should be taken in matters of diet to partake only of digestible foods, and to avoid alcoholic beverages. Plain and nourishing food, and outdoor exercise, with contentment of mind, or love of simplicity of living, are great aids to success. Mental anxiety, or ill health, are not conducive to the desired

end. Attention to correct breathing is of importance."

(A long comment might be added on the necessity of correct breathing, it will perhaps find a place later on in this treatise.)

(7) "As regards the time at which events seen will come to pass, each seer is usually impressed with regard thereto; but as a general rule, visions appearing in the extreme background indicate time more remote, either past or future, than those perceived nearer at hand, while those appearing in the forefront, or close to the seer, denote the present, or immediate future."

(This question of 'time' is an important one, and it is unfortunate that it should largely depend on the 'hunch' of the seer. Time on other planes is differently conditioned, or rather since time is a mode of the human mind, and our mind is at a different state of vibration when examining a vision, the question arises as to the ability of the seer to translate one set of time senses into another corresponding to a different plane. Time in the long run, is discovered to be an illusion after all. There is much in the warning, previously given, that however perfect a vision may appear, it is untrue when brought down to the material plane. More may be said on this matter later.)

CRYSTAL GAZING

(8) "Two principal classes of visions will present themselves to the sitter (a) The Symbolic, indicated by the appearance of symbols such as a flag, boat, knife, gold, etc.: and (b) Actual Scenes and Personages, in action or otherwise."

(In the former instance much will depend on the ability of the seer to translate the symbols correctly, and in the latter there is always liable to be deception by elementals masquerading as the persons that appear to the seer. Remember our warning about the faked book.)

"Persons of a Positive cast of organization, the more active, excitable, yet decided type, are most likely to perceive symbolically or allegorically; while those of a Passive nature usually receive direct or literal revelations. Both classes will find it necessary to carefully cultivate truthfulness, unselfishness, gratitude for what is shown, and absolute confidence in the Love, Wis-dom and Guidance of God Himself."

So ends Mr. Melville's instruction, and he displays his wisdom in thus warning the reader of the necessity of cultivating purity in his own Larger Crystalline Sphere and in relying on nothing but the highest as his ultimate Guide. We shall understand this more clearly as the work progresses, meanwhile enough has been given to enable the would-be seer to start without further delay—his actual practice of the Art.

Follow the above instructions carefully, and perform your first ten-minute practice now, before you go any further in the study of this treatise. Then make up your mind to do the practice *every day* till you have proved for yourself the possibility of obtaining some results by this means.

III

The Universal Crystalline Sphere

THERE is little doubt of the possibility of developing the power to "see things" of an unusual and unlooked for nature, if a certain course of action is persisted in. The drunkard proves this possibility beyond shadow of doubt. But as to the value of what is then perceived, and even the value of what we may perceive as a result of our concentrated attention on the crystal, that requires further consideration, and a careful decision on the part of the would-be seer, as to what he is prepared to accept as truth, and what he is willing to reject as valueless, despite – perhaps – its fascinating appearance.

Here we find ourselves in much deeper waters, but it will be well worth while to give the matter careful consideration, for it is written: "What shall it profit a man if he gain the whole world, and lose his own soul?"

We cannot afford to take any chances of exchanging The Soul – our Greater Crystalline Sphere – for any lesser consideration that may fascinate us by means of reflection in our Glass Globe or Lesser Crystalline Sphere.

Mr. Melville, while pointing out in his little book that the ancient and more elaborate methods of using the Crystal involve a great deal more preparation, and possibly more danger on account of the fact that in olden times the Seers did not use the Crystal so much as a means to personal clairvoyance, as in order to compel the actual presence of certain genii or spirits in the crystal, and to obtain therefrom answers to such questions as might be propounded by the querent rather discounts the value of the more practical application therein implied.

He says "That as the ordinary experimenter of today has no desire to compel the presence of a spiritual being in the crystal, it is quite unnecessary for him or her to draw magic circles, or to go to the trouble and expense of acquiring and using special or costly apparatus, with the exception of the crystal itself." But, after all, let us pay a little attention to what we are doing, before we accept too readily the statement that a certain degree of trouble and expense are un-necessary and the assurance that we can place reliance on the results obtained by the simple method of gazing into the crystal and taking a chance as to what we see presented to our inner vision. The Ancients, generally speaking, were not half so easily deceived as many moderns who dabble in arts and sciences with very little real knowledge as to what they are undertaking or expect as a result.

CRYSTAL GAZING

I can do no better than quote a brief article which appeared in an American Magazine, written by The Master Therion, on:

The Ouija Board.

"Suppose a perfect stranger came into your office and proceeded to give orders to your staff. Suppose a strange woman walked into your drawing room and insisted on being hostess. You would be troubled by this. Yet, people sit down and offer the use of their brains and hands (which are, after all, more important than offices and drawing rooms) to any stray intelligences that may be wandering about. People use the Ouija Board without taking the slightest precautions.

"The establishment of the identity of a spirit by ordinary methods is a very difficult problem, but the majority of people who play at Occultism do not even worry about this, They get something, and it does not seem to matter what! Every inanity, every stupidity, every piece of rubbish, is taken not only on its face value, but at an utterly exaggerated value. The most appallingly bad poetry will pass for Shelly, if only its authentication be that of a planchette! There is, however a good way of using this instrument to get what you want, and that is to perform the whole operation in a consecrated circle, so that undesirable aliens cannot interfere with it. You should then employ the proper magical invocation in order to get into your circle the one spirit that you want. It is comparatively easy to do this. A few simple instructions are all that is necessary, and I shall be pleased to give these, free of charge, to anyone who cares to apply.

"It is not particularly easy to get the spirit of a dead man, because the human soul, being divine, is not amenable to the control of other human souls; and it is further not legitimate or desirable to do it. But what can be done is to pick up the astral remains of the dead man from the Akasha and to build them up into a concrete mind. This operation, again, is not, particularly profitable. The only legitimate work in this line is to get into touch with the really high intelligences, such as we call Gods, Archangels, and the like. These can give real information as to what is most necessary for our progress. And it is written in the Oracles of Zoroaster that unto the Persevering Mortal the Blessed Immortals are swift."

Here, for the case of the Ouija Board applies equally to the Crystal, we find a masterly common-sense explanation of why the ancient and modern adepts resort to more careful, if more elaborate, methods to insure proper results. The danger lies in failure to adopt them, rather than the reverse.

CRYSTAL GAZING

But, after all, we have been considering the crystal chiefly as an aid to the development of our Inner Self, rather than the possibility of Divination by its means. In this course we should persist for the present.

In Melville's work we find a Plate showing the operator seated before his table with his gaze fixed upon the crystal (which being on a stand is nearly at the level of his eyes), while the rays of magnetism, following the line of vision focussed in the eyes, spread out slightly till they reach the crystal, then widely diverge as representing the Universal attraction of the Crystal itself. In other words, The Universal forces and the Human forces meet at the point of the Crystal and thus produce the vision.

Up to this point we had only taken into consideration the Lesser Crystalline Sphere, and the Greater one, or The Soul of Man, but had left out of account the Corresponding Sphere of a Universal Nature. This will be dealt with more fully in its proper place, meanwhile a few words may be said on the *modus operandi* of bringing the enquirer into direct contact with the crystal, and through its medium, with the unseen world. Melville suggests:

"(1) By Concentration in the Crystal of the greatest possible influx of celestial or terrestrial magnetism, or both.

"(2) By Concentration in the Body of the operator of unalloyed magnetism, through the purity of the amatory functions.

"(3) By Concentration of the Mind, through the faculty of "Concentrativeness," acting through the Brain "centre" located in the superior portion of the First Occipital convolution of the Cerebrum."

All the above, it will be seen, imply Concentration, and this is all focused in the Crystal.

The real key to the reference to our "amatory functions" is that we must "fall in love with the object of our work" for Love is the tendency of any two things to become one, thus losing themselves in a third idea, different from either of them. When the experimenter has so concentrated his attention on the *crystal* that no other idea enters his mind, the SEER and the SEEN, as it were, rush together and blend into a vision of a more Universal Order. *Self* and the Crystal are both forgotten when this "marriage" takes place.

Now comes an interesting question. Is it necessary that the crystal or magical link be within sight of the operator at all? Again, may the concentration of the mind of the operator on a point *within* his own being produce similar, perhaps better results? In other words, is the *crystal* but a means towards CONCENTRATION OF MIND, which when accomplished may be better transferred to some other centre or focal point.

In regard to the question of the *magical* link the author may quote one of his own early experiences which may be of interest to some other students.

On May 28th, 1914 between 10:10 and 10:35 P. M. his Magical Record shows that in accordance with instructions received from the great Order of which he was then a Neophyte, he was attempting to answer the following Examination Question from a series of practical questions forming part of the task of his Grade.

"Discover by means of Astral Visions the nature of the Alchemical principles Sulphur, Mercury, and Salt. How do they differ from the Three Gunas and from the Elements Fire, Water and Air?"

Without going into the means of Astral Vision (not the crystal) or the early part of the visions, we may quote the following entry from his record:

> "Thirdly, I considered "Salt" and there came a vision of a ship upon the sea, this ship presently struck a rock and was sucked down into the depths of, the ocean, to rise no more. And I meditated upon this, as the action of Tamas, sloth. Once strike the "Earth" and its "Waters" (or Tamas) will draw you down and hold

you fast, more surely than either the energy of Sulphur or the calm of Mercury."

"May 29th, 1914. Last night, after entering diary about 11:5 P. M. I felt very cold indeed, and went over to the next camp to fetch R. I was still shivering when I went to bed. This morning, at the Railway Station, I heard of the sinking of *The Empress of Ireland*.

"It was not until after my arrival at the office that I remembered the vision I obtained last night, when it suddenly flashed across my mind as a strange coincidence. On further thought I noticed the time (10:15 to 10:30 P. M. Vancouver British Columbia.) exactly corresponded to 2:30 A. M. at Quebec where the time is 4 hours different. The "Empress" went down at 2:30 A. M."

I thought this of sufficient interest from a scientific point of view (although the vision had come to me merely as a Symbol of the Element, Water) to take a little trouble to prove that I had recorded the vision *before* I could possibly have heard of the accident and within 10 minutes of the actual event the other side of the Continent, so I got a friend to fetch my diary from home and to witness the fact of the entry.

Was the thought form produced by the occurrence transmitted to me while in a

CRYSTAL GAZING

receptive state of mind; and had the shivering anything to do with the condition?

Now comes the interesting point. All the above may have been coincidence, but I was interested, some months later, to receive a letter marked *"Recovered by divers from the wreck of the Empress of Ireland"* and returned with the Government stamp to that effect thereon.

This letter turned out to be the one I had written to Fra. 0. M. on May 21st informing him that I was about to commence this series of experiments.

In this instance the letter containing the magnetism of the writer, seems to have been a sufficient link, at a distance of thousands of miles, to produce a symbolic vision of the nature sometimes seen in Crystals.

But it must be remembered that the mind of the Seer chanced at that time to be concentrated, not on the *lesser crystal* but within His Greater Crystalline Sphere, the Astral portion of his Sphere of Sensation. This, in the properly trained Seer, becomes of far greater importance than the *exterior crystal globe,* for although it but *reflects* the Higher Visions, it does *so directly* not by relays. Also it is more like a *Hollow Sphere* at the *CENTRE* of which is the consciousness of the operator. We may now consider how the Ancients looked upon the Universe as to its formation. Their plan does not tally with modern scientific ideas, but

Personal.

VANCOUVER B.C.
MAY 22
10 AM
1914

VANCOUVER
EXHIBITION
SEPT 3-12
1914

Recovered by divers from wreck of S.S. Empress of Ireland.

Frater O. M.
c/o Messrs Wieland & Co.
33 Avenue Studios,
South Kensington.
London. S.W.

ENGLAND.

Figure III

C. STANSFELD JONES
MEMBER OF THE
SOCIETY OF MINIATURISTS.

Post Office Box 70
VANCOUVER.B.C.

May 21st 1914.

Care Frater,

Just a line to acknowledge the receipt of your letter of the 1st inst.,together with my diary, also to thank you for thehelpfull comments and advice.

I am making the necessary preparations to insure a quiet and proper place for the working out of the Examination that has been set for me,and will forward the results as soon as I obtain them.

Until then,I am,
Yours fraternally

Frater O. M.
33 Avenue Studios .
LONDON. S.W.

Unus in Omnibus

Figure II

Fig. II & III

it was probably the result of their own *experience* of Higher Planes, and as before stated, however perfect the Vision it to not true when brought down to this plane.

According to the anonymous author of "The Canon," the cosmos of the Christians, according to late writers, but presumably derived from the tradition of the ancient church, consisted of three principal divisions: First, there were the three circles of the empyreum, secondly, the sphere of the fixed stars, together with the seven planets; and, lastly the sublunary, or elementary world.

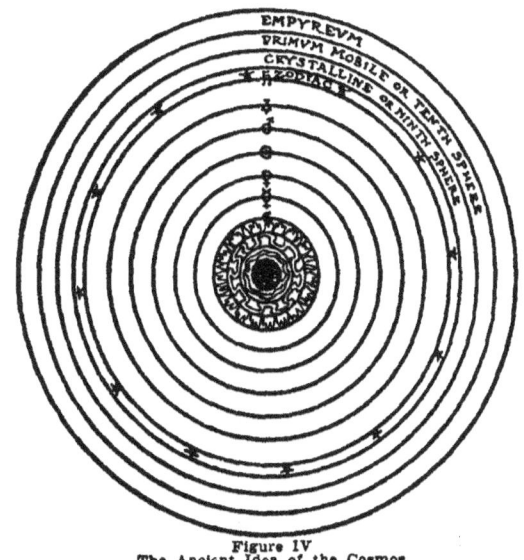

Figure IV
The Ancient Idea of the Cosmos

At the Centre of their conception is the Earth, or Elementary Kingdom, around which circled the Moon. Outside this, is a series of concentric spheres of the Planetary Influences. First Mercury, then Venus, The Sun, Mars, Jupiter and Saturn, beyond which great sphere is to be found that of the Zodiac or Star Universe. But outside that again is what they conceived as The Crystalline Sphere, as it were the Magic Mirror of Heaven about which was the Primum Mobile or Whirling Motion and Finally the Great Unknown Empyreum.

If we can get but a faint conception of this Universal Crystalline Sphere, we shall be well repaid for the trouble and pains we may be at to accomplish this. In order that we may attain to that Perfect Clear Vision, known to the Adepts, we must learn to receive the Light of this Universal Sphere in the Crystal Soul of our own being, thus obtaining true Knowledge of the Higher Self, and finally of God and The Universe.

We may well stand in awe before the greatness of this conception, as compared - perhaps - with the aims we set out to accomplish at the beginning of our practice. Yet "The soul of man is immortal, and its future Is the future of a thing whose growth and splendour have no limit. The principle that gives life dwells In us, and without us, is undying and eternally beneficent, is not heard or seen or felt, but is perceived by the man who desires perception.

CRYSTAL GAZING

Each man is his own absolute law-giver, the dispenser of glory or gloom to himself, the decreer of his life, his reward, his punishment." (Idyll of the White Lotus).

And we, each and every one, must choose for him or herself, whether we linger on the way, or with untiring effort press onward to the true goal of Clear Vision.

IV

A Consideration of the Ancient Methods

THE ENQUIRER, having read thus far, will have realized that behind and beyond all that he may hitherto have considered as the Art of Crystal Gazing, there is a Greater and Wider field of application, making necessary more careful preparations, but leading to correspondingly important results. At this point it will be necessary for him, or her, to decide whether or not they are prepared to carry the practice beyond the preliminary stages already described, and in case they desire to do so, they must be ready to fulfill the necessary requirements.

We should first consider the best of the ancient instructions available, and later, we may be able to find points in which they seem inadequate, and others that can certainly be improved upon.

The Methods of Trithemius of Spanheim - The Friend and Teacher of Cornelius Agrippa - who lived in the Sixteenth Century, as transmitted to us by Francis Barrett, who translated his work from the Latin in the early part of the Nineteenth Century, have been considered the clearest and best of their kind. We find parts of these instructions quoted in practically all the books on the subject that have been published since, sometimes with acknowledgments and sometimes without.

A few fragments of Barrett's Introduction to that work, written by him in the form of a letter to a young friend and fellow Student, may not be out of place here, since the advice then given, holds equally good at this day.

> My Friend:
> Knowing thee to be a curious searcher after those sciences which are out of the common track of study, (I mean the art of foretelling events, magic, talismans, etc.) I am moved spiritually to give thee my thoughts upon them, and by these ideas here written, to open to thine eye (spiritual) as much information as it seems necessary for thee to know, by which thou mayest be led by the hand into the delectable field of nature; and to give thee such documents as, guided by the supreme wisdom of the Highest, thou mayest refresh thy soul with a delicious draught of knowledge; so that after recreating thy spirit with the use of those good gifts which may please God to bestow upon thee, thou mayest be wrapped up into the contemplation of the immense wisdom of that great munificent Being who created thee.
>
> Now, thou art a man in whose soul the image of Divinity is sealed for eternity, think first what is thy desire in searching

CRYSTAL GAZING

after these mysteries? Is it wealth, honour, fame, power, might, aggrandizement, and the like? Perhaps thy heart says, All I all these I would gladly crave! If so, this is my answer, - seek first to know thyself thoroughly, cleanse thy heart from all wicked, vain and rapacious desires.

To know thyself is to know God, for it is the spiritual gift from. God that enables a man to know himself. This gift but very few possess, as may be daily seen.

Seek ye first the kingdom of God, and all things shall be added unto you.

Farewell, remember my poor counsel, and be happy.

F. B.

Of The Making Of The Crystal, And The Form Of Preparation For A Vision.

Procure of a lapidary good clear pellucid crystal, of the bigness of a small orange i.e. about one inch and a half in diameter; let it be globular or round each way alike; then when you have got this crystal, fair and clear, without any clouds or specks, get a small plate of pure gold to encompass the crystal round one-half; let this be fitted on an ivory or ebony pedestal, as you may see more fully described in the drawing (see Frontispiece). Let there be engraved a circle round the crystal with these characters around inside the circle, next the crystal: A Hexagram, a Pentagram and a Maltese Cross; afterwards the name "Tetragrammaton". On the other side of the plate let there be engraved "Michael, Gabriel, Uriel, Raphael;" which are the four principal angels ruling over the Sun, Moon, Venus and Mercury; but on the table on which the crystal stands, the following names, characters, etc., must be drawn in order.

First, the names of the seven planets and angels ruling them, with their seals and characters. The names of the four kings of the four corners of the earth. Let them be all written within a double circle, with a triangle on a table; on which plate the crystal on its pedestal: this being done, thy table is complete (as in Frontispiece) and fit for the calling of the spirits; after which thou shalt proceed to experiment thus. (*See Figure I*).

In what time thou wouldest, deal with the spirits by the table and crystal, thou must observe the planetary hour: and whatsoever planet rules that hour, the angel governing the planet thou shalt call in the manner following; but first, say this short prayer.

"Oh God! who art the author of all good things, strengthen, I beseech thee, thy poor servant, that he may stand fast, without fear, through this dealing and work: enlighten, I

The Magic Instruments of Art
Figure I

beseech thee, oh Lord, the dark understanding of thy creature, so that his spiritual eye may be opened to see and know thy angelic spirits descending here in this crystal: (Then lay thy hand on the crystal saying,) and thou, oh inanimate creature of God, be sanctified and consecrated, and blessed to this purpose, that no evil phantasy may appear in thee; or, if they do gain ingress into this creature, they may be constrained to speak intelligibly, and truly, and without the least ambiguity, for Christ's sake. Amen.

"And forasmuch as thy servant here standing before thee, oh Lord! desires neither evil treasure, nor injury to his neighbor, nor hurt to any living creature, grant him the power of descrying those celestial spirits or intelligences, that may appear in this crystal, and whatever good gifts (whether the power of healing infirmities, or of imbibing wisdom, or discovering any evil likely to afflict any person or family, or any other gift) thou mayest be pleased to bestow on me, enable me, by thy wisdom and mercy, to use whatever I may receive to the honour of thy holy name. Grant this for thy son Christ's sake. Amen."

Then taking your ring and pentacle, put the ring on the little finger of your right hand; hang the pentacle round thy neck; (Note, the pentacle may be either written on clean virgin parchment, or engraven on a square plate of silver and suspended from thy neck to the

CRYSTAL GAZING

breast), then take your black ebony wand with the gilt characters on it and trace the circle, saying, "In the name of the blessed Trinity, I consecrate this piece of ground for our defense; so that no evil spirit may have power to break these bonds prescribed here, through Jesus Christ our Lord." Amen.

Then place the vessel for the perfumes between thy circle and the holy table on which the crystal stands, and, having fire therein, cast in thy perfumes, saying.

"I conjure thee, oh thou creature of fire! by him who created all things both in heaven and earth, and in the sea, and in every other place whatever, that forthwith thou cast away every phantasm from thee, that no hurt whatsoever shall be done in anything. Bless, oh Lord, this creature of fire, and sanctify it that it may be blessed, and that they may fill up the power and virtue of their odours; so neither the enemy, nor any false imagination may enter into them; through our Lord Jesus Christ. Amen."

Now, this being done in the order prescribed, take thy little book, which must be made about seven inches long, of pure white virgin vellum or paper, likewise pen and ink must be ready to write down the name, character, and office, likewise the seal or image of whatever spirit may appear (for this I must tell you that it does not happen that the same spirit you call will always appear, for you must try the spirit to know whether he be a pure or impure being, and this thou shalt easily know by a firm and undoubted faith in God).

Now the most pure and simple way of calling the spirits or spirit is by a short oration to the spirit himself, which is more effectual and easy to perform than composing a table of letters; for all celestial operations, the more pure and unmixed they are, the more they are agreeable to the celestial spirits: therefore, after the circle is drawn, the book, perfumes, rod, etc., in readiness, proceed as follows:

(After noticing the exact hour of the day, and what angel rules that hour, thou shalt say.)

"In the name of the blessed and holy Trinity, I do desire thee, thou strong and mighty angel Michael (or any other angel or spirit), that if it be the divine will of him who is called Tetragrammaton, etc., the Holy God, the Father, that thou take upon thee some shape as best beseemeth thy celestial nature, and appear to us visibly here in this crystal, and answer our demands in as far as we shall not transgress the bounds of the divine mercy and goodness, by requesting unlawful knowledge; but that thou will graciously shew us what things are most profitable for us to know and do, to the glory and honour of his divine

CRYSTAL GAZING

Majesty, who liveth and reigneth, world without end. Amen.

"Lord, thy will be done on earth, as it is in heaven: -make clean our hearts within us, and take not thy Holy Spirit from us.

"Lord, by thy name, we have called him, suffer him to administer unto us. And that all things may work together for thy honour and glory, to whom with thee, the Son, and blessed Spirit be ascribed all might, majesty and dominion. Amen."

Note, In these dealings, two should always be present; for often a spirit is manifest to one in the crystal when the other cannot perceive him; therefore if any spirit appear, as there most likely will, to one or both say,

"Oh Lord! we return thee our hearty and sincere thanks for the hearing of our prayer, and we thank thee for having permitted thy spirit to appear unto us which we, by thy mercy, will interrogate to our further instruction, through Christ. Amen.

Interrog. 1. In the name of the holy and undefiled Spirit, the Father, the begotten Son, and Holy Ghost, proceeding from both, what is thy true name?

If the spirit answers, Michael, then proceed.

Question 2. What is thy office? 3. What is thy true sign or character? 4. When are the times most agreeable to thy nature to hold conference with us?

Wilt thou swear by the blood and righteousness of our Lord Jesus Christ, that thou art truly Michael?

(Let him swear, then write down his seal or character in thy book, and against it, his office and times to be called, through God's name; also write down anything he may teach thee, or any responses he may make to thy questions or interrogations, concerning life or death, arts or sciences, or any other thing) ; and then thou shalt say,

"Thou great and mighty spirit, inasmuch as thou camest in peace and in the name of the ever blessed and righteous Trinity, so in this name thou mayest depart, and return to us when we call thee in his name to whom every knee doth bow down. Fare thee well, Michael; peace be between us, through our blessed Lord Jesus Christ. Amen."

Then will the spirit depart; then say, "To God the Father, eternal Spirit, fountain of Light, the Son, and Holy Ghost, be all honour and glory, world without end. Amen.

I shall here set down the Table of the names of Spirits and Planets governing the Hours; so thou shalt easily know by inspection, what Spirit and Planet governs every Hour of the Day and night in the Week.

Hours Day	Angels and Planets ruling Sunday	Angels and Planets ruling Monday	Angels and Planets ruling Tuesday	Angels and Planets ruling Wednesday
	Day	Day	Day	Day
1	Michael	Gabriel	Samael	Raphael
2	Anael	Cassiel	Michael	Gabriel
3	Raphael	Sachiel	Anael	Cassiel
4	Gabriel	Samael	Raphael	Sachiel
5	Cassiel	Michael	Gabriel	Samael
6	Sachiel	Anael	Cassiel	Michael
7	Samael	Raphael	Sachiel	Anael
8	Michael	Gabriel	Samael	Raphael
9	Anael	Cassiel	Michael	Gabriel
10	Raphael	Sachiel	Anael	Cassiel
11	Gabriel	Samael	Raphael	Sachael
12	Cassiel	Michael	Gabriel	Samael

Hours Night	Night	Night	Night	Night
1	Sachiel	Anael	Cassiel	Michael
2	Samael	Raphael	Sachiel	Anael
3	Michael	Gabriel	Samael	Raphael
4	Anael	Cassiel	Michael	Gabriel
5	Raphael	Sachiel	Anael	Cassiel
6	Gabriel	Samael	Raphael	Sachiel
7	Cassiel	Michael	Gabriel	Samael
8	Sachiel	Anael	Cassiel	Michael
9	Samael	Raphael	Sachiel	Anael
10	Michael	Gabriel	Samael	Raphael
11	Anael	Cassiel	Michael	Gabriel
12	Raphael	Sachiel	Anael	Cassiel

Hours Day	Angels and Planets ruling Thursday	Angels and Planets ruling Friday	Angels and Planets ruling Saturday
	Day	Day	Day
1	Sachiel	Anael	Cassiel
2	Samael	Raphael	Sachiel
3	Michael	Gabriel	Samael
4	Anael	Cassiel	Michael
5	Raphael	Sachiel	Anael
6	Gabriel	Samael	Raphael
7	Cassiel	Michael	Gabriel
8	Sachiel	Anael	Cassiel
9	Samael	Raphael	Sachiel
10	Michael	Gabriel	Samael
11	Anael	Cassiel	Michael
12	Raphael	Sachiel	Anael

Hours Night	Night	Night	Night
1	Gabriel	Samael	Raphael
2	Cassiel	Michael	Gabriel
3	Sachiel	Anael	Cassiel
4	Samael	Raphael	Sachiel
5	Michael	Gabriel	Samael
6	Anael	Cassiel	Michael
7	Raphael	Sachiel	Anael
8	Gabriel	Samael	Raphael
9	Cassiel	Michael	Gabriel
10	Sachiel	Anael	Cassiel
11	Samael	Raphael	Sachiel
12	Michael	Gabriel	Samael

FRATER ACHAD

Note, the day is divided into twelve equal parts, called planetary hours, reckoning from sun-rise to sun-set and, again, from the setting to the rising; and to find the planetary hour, you need but to divide the natural hours by twelve, and the quotient gives the length of the planetary hours and odd minutes, which shows you how long a spirit bears rule in that day; as Michael governs the first and the eighth hour on Sunday, as does the Sun. After you have the length, of the first hour, you have only to look in the table, as if it be the fourth hour, on Sunday, you see in the Table that the Moon and Gabriel rules; and so for the rest it being so plain and easy you cannot err."

This concludes the Ancient Instruction.

Although at first reading the above instructions may appear comparatively simple, as in fact they are, the student will soon find that a great deal of further information is desirable, and necessary in order to obtain a thorough practical grasp of the matter. The more astute will discover that a much wider knowledge of Magick and Occultism is implied, than is possessed by the average reader. Herein lies the difficulty of the present author, who, while desirous of being really helpful to earnest Students, knows clearly the obstacles to the practical application of this method of working.

CRYSTAL GAZING

For instance, we have been supplied with details whereby we may appear to stand a fair chance of invoking the Angel Michael (always provided our intentions are pure, and we are of that simple Religious turn of mind, prepared be believe implicitly in the instructions and the Powers Invoked, without questioning the reason why things are thus and so and not otherwise), but Michael is but one of the seven Angels mentioned in the table of Planets and Rulers, and his services are only at our disposal at intervals.

In order to be in a position to invoke the Angels of the other hours and Planets, we must be in possession of their Names in Hebrew, together with their Sigils or Characters, and these must be Written on the Circle and Table in place of those given in the Plate. Also, in place of the Symbol of The Sun, on the rim of the Circle, must be placed the proper Planetary Symbol corresponding to the Angel Invoked; and so on.

Nor do our difficulties end here, for we may ask why the Sigil (that peculiar figure placed under the name Michael within the Hexagon on the Table, and on the upper left hand side of the Circle) should be that of Michael, and no other. In order to answer this, the methods of drawing the Sigils of Angels, Intelligences, and Spirits, from their Magic

Squares, or by other means, would need explanation.

Magick is in truth the Science of Life itself, and all things in True Magick have a perfectly clear and lucid explanation, each step has a definite connection with the one before and the one following. But that is where the practical difficulty comes in; we want to learn Crystal Gazing, and we find that before we can do anything with the matter properly, we must have learned many other things, in order to be in position even to carry out such a simple Ceremony as above described. On the other hand, if things are (apparently) made too easy for us, we fail to understand the underlying principles involved, and through failure to obtain a proper grasp of the matter, we are led into a condition where, instead of us having the proper Power and Authority over the spirit invoked, IT has power over us, and since we have no means of TESTING its true NATURE, we may easily be deceived, led into further error, and finally lost.

Every Divine Name, for instance, on the Circle or Holy Table shown in the Plate, has a very definite meaning, and is placed just where it is for a very definite reason. To the Magician, who understands every detail, these form the best and only true PROTECTION, since he USES these things as his instruments and relies on his power to use

CRYSTAL GAZING

them rightly. To the novice or uninitiate, they mean little or nothing, and how can he USE things he understands nothing about. Of course the fact that he must procure even these few simple materials, and fashion them properly, gives him a certain knowledge of the matter, but a very superficial one. And these articles are not so easily procured as one might imagine.

Take for instance "The Black Ebony Wand" shown in the illustration, which we are told to engrave with certain Names and Figures. If made, what will this wand mean to us?

It may mean a stick of wood, without life, and little more than a walking-stick (if as much), or it may represent our Highest and Most Divine Possession.

The True Wand is the Divine Will in Man, and one who is thus able to exercise the Divine Will, may certainly be in a position to use it to Consecrate a Circle. The Wand here described is a Symbol of that Will and to prepare it we must have gone through a Ceremony very like the one described in the First Chapter of this Book, in regard to the Crystal, but much more powerful, since we are dealing with our chief Magical Weapon. Why is the Wand Black? To represent perfect Understanding on the part of the Instrument, and perfect absorption of the Will of the Operator, which in turn is God's Will. It thus forms a veritable "Hollow Tube to bring down fire from Heaven". Again its substance is rigid and unbending ebony to represent the Power of Unconquered Will. Engraved upon it are the Words of Power AGLA-ON-TETRAGRAMMATON, and on the reverse side EGO ALPHA ET OMEGA. What is the meaning of this to one who realizes the nature of the Wand? AGLA is a Word of Power, the Initials of which form the sentence "Ateh Geburah le-Olahm Adonai" which means "Unto Thee be the Power 0 My Lord Adonai" thus asserting the Power of Adonai, The Higher Self of Man (and of Humanity) as Lord of All. The next Word, ON, is the Name of the SUN in the old Egyptian Language, and the Sun again represents The Power on High giving Life to all beings on this planet; again it has a correspondence in ourselves, as, the Human Will situated in the Heart, etc.

TETRAGRAMMATON, means the Four Lettered Name, the Ineffable Name IHVH, having Power over all the Elements, and representing the complete FORMULA of the MAGICK SYSTEM here used. The words on the reverse side "EGO ALPHA ET OMEGA" mean "I am Alpha and Omega, the Beginning and the End, the first and the Last" thus asserting the Wand or True Will to be supreme, and also containing the Greek formula of IAO, which is similar to that of Tetragrammaton.

CRYSTAL GAZING

This will give the Student some idea of what is involved in even such an apparently simple set of Magical Instruments as is here depicted. Is he prepared to assert his Will as the Will of God and the Universe? If not, he is not ready to acquire and use the Wand. So it is with the other instruments, about which a long treatise might be written, most useful and interesting to the few earnest Students, but quite beyond the comprehension of the ordinary reader.

It would give the Author great pleasure to write such a treatise around the simple ceremony above described, but the limits of this little book will not permit. Should a real demand arise, it will no doubt become possible for the real student to obtain the information necessary. For it is written "When the Pupil is ready the Master appears."

V

Further Considerations –
The Methods of Dr. Dee and Sir Edward Kelly

THERE is one point the Student may, or may not, have noticed in regard to the Simple Ceremony described in the previous chapter, viz: the entire absence of any ceremony of Purification or Banishing.

This may be accounted for by the fact that the Operator is supposed to be one who has implicit faith and trust in the Divine Powers Invoked, but it is only the Purest and Highest type of Seer who can safely use these methods, and at the same time, their simplicity is likely to attract the most ignorant.

A little knowledge is a dangerous thing, and Magick either requires a great deal of knowledge, or *none at all,* and when we say *None at all* we mean Knowledge must have been transcended and have given place to Understanding or Direct Perception.

There are proper Ceremonies for Banishing and Invoking which should be used whenever a Circle is used in an operation of this sort. Again, to understand them rightly requires considerable work on the part of the Student.

It is not my intention to discourage the beginner from an attempt to put into practice any part of this Art, which however is also a Science. No Science can be learned in a day, and unless the Scientific aspect be first mastered, how can one be in a position to carry out the practical side in a skillful manner, befitting any of the Arts.

A few words should be written on the necessity of Banishing before undertaking any Occult or Magical Work. When we first of all dealt with our crystal, we found it necessary to Banish from it any impure Astral Influences that might have been present within it, after which we Consecrated it, and Charged it with our Will. It is equally necessary, therefore, that in the event of our desiring to Work within a Magic Circle, drawn on the floor of our Temple, (or Room) we should first banish all impure influences from that room, or at least cause them to remain outside the circle, which in this case is but symbolical of the universal crystalline sphere from which we desire to call down influence upon our lesser crystalline sphere, and in turn to be able to comprehend them, by means of a vision, within our own crystal sphere – the soul.

If this Soul is Pure and Clear in the first instance, nothing can harm it, but usually the practices we undertake are for the purpose of purifying our own vehicle.

CRYSTAL GAZING

The burning of incense may help to purify the atmosphere in our surroundings, but this incense itself is impure until it has been *PURIFIED* and *CONSECRATED* *to* the work in hand. This at least we may accomplish, by methods very similar to those adopted in the case of the crystal. A more elaborate preparation is certainly advisable, but this is not the place to enter into full details of the Banishing Rituals of the Pentagram and Hexagram. These details may be found in "The Equinox." Vol. I Number 2 by those who need them sufficiently to feel it worth while to obtain them.

The practical importance, however, of these Rituals cannot be overrated. They form a means of Banishing all that is undesirable in our surroundings, Elementary, Planetary and Zodiacal; and also of invoking the Powers of the Elements, Planets and Signs in the proper way.

The failure to understand these things has led in the past to many disastrous results; and the world today seems blissfully ignorant of even the necessity of any such performance, while at the same time attempting to deal with "Phenomena" of a Spiritualistic Type, which in many instances is nearer to the necromantic results of Evocation than the comparatively safe methods of Invocation described in the last chapter.

FRATER ACHAD

We may now turn our attention to some of the possible results of Crystal Gazing, when undertaken in the right manner. This, at least, may encourage the enquirer to "make himself fit" to accomplish similar results in time.

Few people realize what an important factor the Crystal has played, and is playing, in events of Planetary Importance concerning the Initiation of the whole of Humanity. It seems a far cry from the practice of Crystal Gazing to the New Aeon, but it may be there is more than a slight connection even in that instance. In any case, the practice may lead to results far greater than ever imagined in the beginning, and these results may only become manifest long after the original seer has passed away and is almost forgotten.

In any case it is doubtful whether the old Abbot Trithemius of Spanheim dreamed that his instructions, written so long ago, were going to be copied and commented upon in this little book, or could have foreseen – any more than the present author can foresee – the result upon the lives of those who may read them and act upon them in the future.

In the latter part of the Sixteenth and early part of the Seventeenth Centuries, there lived another man, to whom the Art of Crystal Gazing came to mean much. I refer to Dr. Dee who during his Occult career made the acquaintance of a certain Crystal Gazer known as Edward Kelly. The result of their work is certainly active today, and had it not been for them, it is very doubtful if the present treatise would ever have been written.

Quoting from a recently published *Life of John Dee* by Charlotte Fell Smith (although this book is not of great practical importance to the Student) we obtain the following:

The Crystal Gazers

It is a curious picture to call up, that of the strangely assorted pair seated in the inner room at Mortlake, acting out this spiritual drama. Dee had asked for instructions about the room for the sittings:

"May my little farthest chamber serve, if the bed be taken down?" The table, covered with its cloth, stood in the centre upon the seals. Kelly, perhaps with the black cap he is credited with having always worn, pulled close over his ears, was seated at it. Dee at his desk sat writing in the great folio book. He was now fifty-six years old; his beard was long, but perhaps not yet 'as white as milk' as Aubrey describes it. He did not apparently see the visions himself. Once he reproachfully said: 'You know I cannot see or skry'. He conversed with the spirits and sometimes heard what they said; but to the eye and ear of his body they were invisible; hence his dependence upon a skryer.

"The sole object of his ambition was the attainment of legitimate wisdom. When conversing with the angels, how near within his grasp it seemed! Michael's exposition seemed almost to promise it to him:

"'Wilt thou have witt and wisdom? Here it is.

"Michael points each time to a figure of seven squares shown within a circle of light.

"'The exaltation and government of princes is in my hand.

"'In counsayle and Nobilitie, I prevayle.

"'The Gayne and Trade of Merchandise is in my hand. Lo I here it is.

"'The Qualitie of the Earth and Waters is my knowledge, and I know them. And here it is.

"'The motion of the Ayre and those that move in it, are all known to me. Lo! here they are.

"'I signifie wisdom. In fire is my government, I was in the beginning and shall be to the end.

"'Mark these mysteries. For this knowne, the state of the whole earth is knowne, and all that is thereon. Mighty is God, yea, mighty is he who hath composed forever. Give diligent eye. Be wise, merry and pleasant in the *Lord*.'"

CRYSTAL GAZING

Here we have one of the communications from the Angel Michael that has been Historically recorded. In fact a great deal of the work of Dee and Kelly remains in actual writing to this day. Many of their formulae are being used by the true Adepts, and much work has yet to be done in order to make the meaning of this early work entirely clear. The public knows little or nothing of all this, but I may quote from certain Official Instructions of The Great White Brotherhood or A. A. which deals with the matter.

"The Skryer (Edward Kelly) obtained from certain Angels a series of seven talismans. These, grouped about the Holy Twelvefold Table, similarly obtained, were part of the furniture of the Holy Table."

"Other Pantacles were obtained in a similar manner. Here (Figure V) is the principal one, which carved in wax, was placed upon the top of the table. On four others stood the feet of the table.

$$\text{SAAI} \tfrac{21}{8} \text{EME}$$
$$\text{BTZKASE}^{30}$$
$$\text{HEIDENE}$$
$$\text{DEIMOL}^{30}\text{A}$$
$$\text{I}_{26}\text{MEGCBE}$$
$$\text{ILAOI} \tfrac{21}{8} \text{VN}$$
$$\text{IHRLAAL} \tfrac{21}{8}$$

"Note first the Holy Sevenfold Table containing seven Names of God which not even the Angels are able to pronounce.

"These names are seen written without the heptagram within the heptagon."

This Holy Sevenfold Table is probably the one referred to by the Angel Michael in the communication above quoted. It forms the Key to manifold and great Mysteries.

By reading these obliquely are obtained the names of other sets of Angels, some of which were attributed to the Metals of the Planets, as also by other methods of reading can be obtained the Names of the Seven Great Angels, etc., etc. All the names of the Angels thus drawn from the Sevenfold Table appear on the Pantacle or SIGILLUM DEI AEMETH.

THE SIGILLUM DEI AEMETH, A PANTACLE
MADE BY DR. JOHN DEE
Figure V

CRYSTAL GAZING

Dr. Dee also had a *Shew-stone,* a crystal which he alleged, to have been brought to him by angels. This was placed upon the Table, and the principal result of the ceremonial skrying of Sir Edward Kelly, was the obtaining of a series of wonderful diagrams, containing the Keys to all the mysteries of the Universe.

He symbolized the Fourth-Dimensional Universe in two dimensions as a square surrounded by 30 concentric circles, (known as the 30 Aethyrs or Aires) whose radii increase in geometrical proportion.

The sides of the square formed Four Great Watch-Towers which are attributed to the elements, these in turn are all governed by what is known as "The Table of Union", attributed to Spirit.

Dr. Dee also obtained the Alphabet of the Angelic Language, in which all these my-steries were written. It is sometimes called the Enochian Alphabet, as the angels claimed to be those which conversed with the "patriarch Enoch" of Jewish fable.

The Thirty Aires or Aethyrs, surrounding the Material Universe, each had their special name, drawn from these pantacles. Also the names of their Governors were drawn from the same sources. Each of the Aethyrs had three governors, and these in turn controlled from two to nine thousand servitors.

FRATER ACHAD

A series of Forty-eight *Calls* or Invocations were also obtained in the Angelic Language, and by means of these it became possible to Invoke to Visible Appearance all these Aethyric Spheres, with their Angel Guard-ians. This gives but a slight idea of the extent of the practical Magical work done by Dee and Kelly by means of the Crystal or Shew-Stone.

This work has formed the basis of much of the Magical Work of the Adepts of this present time, and was instrumental in bringing about what we now know as The New Aeon. Almost all will now have recognized that we are living in a New Age or Era, and the Magical Forces which have brought this about, are largely due, in the first instance, to the *Keys* to the Higher Spheres obtained by Dee and Kelly, some centuries before Humanity was ripe for the actual Initiating of the Current of Higher Will, which the practical use of these Keys made possible in this age.

All this may sound highly fantastical to those who have no initiated knowledge of the Universe, or of the nature and powers of Man. We do not wish to labor the point, but it illustrates how important the Crystal may become in the hands of a true Seer.

The Real Prophet is one who has also the Power to make his prophesies come true. That is the difference between the Major and the Minor Prophets. In this instance many

CRYSTAL GAZING

things *seen* by Dee and Kelly are coming true, but chiefly because a greater Adept than either of them, grasped the possibilities of their Visions and by his Mighty Will, put the necessary Forces into action. We may now consider what is meant by a *Shew-Stone*.

This, in the instance above cited, consisted not in a crystal sphere placed upon a stand on the table, but in a *stone* pressed to the forehead of the Seer. At least such was the material means used in obtaining the Visions of the 30 Aethyrs by Frater 0. M. just before and after The Equinox of the Gods which occurred in 1904 E. V.

In that instance a great Topaz, set in a Scarlet Cross, was used. The process was somewhat different from ordinary crystal-gazing, as likewise were the results.

The place of what is known as the "Third Eye" in man, is just above and between the exterior organs of sight. This is known in Hindu Systems as the "Ajna Chakra" and is thought by some to correspond to the Pineal Gland.

Intense concentration on this "Lotus" or "Chakra" produces Visions of a very high character, and this concentration may be increased or aided-by the pressure of a *skew-stone* to the forehead just over this "third-eye."

In that case the Vision is turned inwards towards the Ajna Chakra, instead of concentrated on an outside object such as the crystal. When the power of concentration has been developed by means of crystal-gazing (as described in the earlier chapters of this book) this concentration may be taken up by the interior organs of vision, and the visions perceived, not in physical space, but in the chitakasha or mental space. Visions of this nature are usually of much greater value than the others which result from our early practices with the eyes open.

Consideration of Visions of this type, as of the proper means of obtaining them, will lead us well on the path to obtaining true Crystal Vision. Since, however, it forms a different aspect of the Work, it will be best to treat of it in another Chapter.

VI

The Attainment of Crystal Vision

THE reader will by now have realized that there is a certain difference between Visions obtained by means of the Crystal, and the attainment of Crystal Vision.

Let us consider the matter in greater detail. If we use a crystal as a means of obtaining visions of what, to us, would otherwise remain unseen, we accomplish our purpose through learning to *concentrate our attention* on the Lesser Crystalline Sphere. Just what we see by this means is beyond our power of control, for we have taken no steps to insure any particular type of vision appearing before us in the crystal. The visions so obtained may be pleasant, or unpleasant; symbolical or actual; past, present, or future; and we have to rely upon our own power of comprehension and our own intuitive ideas, in order to make such visions of value.

Also, the power to see such visions at all, largely depends on our own inner state of development. If we have not been living on the right diet, if we have not learned to breathe correctly, if our own ideas are not of the greatest purity; these visions may be coloured by our own thought, or we may not be able to get beyond the very early stages.

Much therefore depends upon ourselves, and we must be prepared to so train ourselves that these "inner powers", which enable us to contact the subtle vibrations concentrated on the crystal from the Universal Sphere, may become apparent to our conscious mind.

The concentration of our gaze on the crystal is Perhaps the most important part of the whole operation, for we are thus learning to *concentrate our minds* on a single idea.

Concentration of mind leads to the highest results, if rightly directed. It is a valuable acquirement and well worth the time and trouble it may take in order to secure it.

The true Student will probably realize that this power of mental concentration is of greater importance than the mere elementary visions seen in the crystal while we are learning to acquire it., The practices we have undertaken to that end will have served to strengthen the will and with that strengthening of the will comes more power of choice. We are no longer content to remain slaves to our visions (or to our thoughts) we seek a conscious mastery over these things.

In that case, we may begin to question the truth of our visions. We may find ourselves in a position to see certain events which have transpired, or are transpiring, or will transpire

CRYSTAL GAZING

on this material plane. We may follow our *inner guidance* when we interpret these visions, and we may make a true guess, so that what we have beheld may prove in line with fact. On the other hand, we may find many instances when our interpretation of the Symbols, or the Time, connected with our visions is far from correct. Many people forget about these things, and we only hear of the few instances when everything turns out correctly.

Some persons seem naturally gifted with "second sight" and are able to give others an accurate "reading" in a fairly large percentage of cases. But such persons are comparatively rare, and in any case they represent the "mediumistic" passive type of individuals, who are little better than reflectors, with no creative powers of their own.

Crystal gazing, should teach us to become more positive, rather than more negative. Our only chance of true advancement lies in the direction *of control* of the Astral Plane. If we let it control us, we are lost.

The Ancients, realizing this, devised the proper methods for obtaining visions *of a definite type,* or at least from a *definite type of intelligence,* represented – in the examples previously given – by certain Angels of a high order. Such Beings are capable of teaching us great truths, while the mere elementals, with which we may come in contact by less scientific methods, are only too likely to lead us astray.

But we also discovered that in order to carry out the instructions of the Wise Seers of the past, we must first be in possession of a fund of knowledge which would put us in the position to work in an intelligent manner. Should we, on the other hand neglect to obtain this, we should still be just as much at the mercy of the elementary forces, since in our ignorance, we could be easily deceived, and having no means of testing the accuracy of our results, might well come to grief.

Our safest method, therefore, will be to treat every result as *subjective,* as something arising within ourselves, and to leave on one side the question of the *objective reality of* any of our visions. Just because we perceive a "vision" which appears to be in objective space, because we have our physical eyes open and have been gazing at a Crystal, it does not prove that this vision is really outside of us. As a matter of fact all we perceive in the physical universe, is *within* our organ of vision, and the outside cause may be quite other than that which we think it is. A table, for instance, appears as it does on account of certain vibrations from the "outside" entering our consciousness through the "eye" and our inner organ of vision reacts, and projects into

CRYSTAL GAZING

"space" the image that we call a "table". Just what a "table" is in reality, we really do not know.

In any case, when we have been gazing at the crystal, after the mist has cleared away and we become conscious of the "vision", we are not at the same time conscious of our material surroundings.

So we see, that after all, our own "vision" needs to be trained, and that is the most important consideration for the true Seer.

Now, although it is not so easy perhaps, we are just as well able – with practice– to concentrate our minds *inwards* as *outwards*. We can make a *mental picture* of a crystal or some other simple object, and concentrate on that *mental image* while our physical eyes are closed. We have, in other words a certain power of *inner vision* which may be much developed. Once we have learned to concentrate the mind to some extent, we may arouse, by means of our *creative imagination* any kind of vision we desire. But again we cannot be sure that we *imagine truly*, this, however, need not concern us very much for the moment.

If we try to imagine, for instance, a "Red Triangle" we find our mental picture, even of this simple object, trying to escape us. It will change colour, and shape, and size; and at first it is very little under our control. But it is slightly under our control because we created it by means of our will *to perceive a red triangle.* It is quite unlike an idea which *takes possession of our mind* against our will, and obsesses us. Also, the more we practice, the more vividly shall we be able to see the Red Triangle, and the less it will change colour and shape, till one day after we have been practicing a long time, perhaps – we shall be able to *hold it before our mental vision at* will. The fact that we are able to do this, will imply that we have been able to *cut away from consciousness* every other thought except the Red Triangle. What will be the result? There will be a "rushing together of the Seer and the Seen" and in a moment we shall find ourselves in an *entirely new state of consciousness.* Our mind – for a brief period at any rate – will become CRYSTAL CLEAR. We shall have obtained, what in Raja Yoga is called, Dhyana. This is but the first of the Great results, but it is a thousand times more glorious, and more worth while, than any vision in *the crystal* that might have been obtained by concentration of the mind *outside* instead of inside our own Crystalline Sphere.

Again, man has the power – once he has learned to concentrate – to form for himself a "Body of Light" or "Astral Body" which at first surrounds his physical body, and may afterwards be separated from it, so that – while still retaining his full consciousness – he may

CRYSTAL GAZING

learn to *travel* clothed in his Body of Light, on the Astral Plane. He may visit other spheres, those depicted in the Diagram as surrounding the physical world, governed by the planetary intelligences. He may extend his field of knowledge further and further, until some day, if he has succeeded in purifying himself sufficiently in the meanwhile, he may gaze upon that *Universal Crystalline Sphere,* mentioned in our Third Chapter.

It was such a course that Frater 0. M. took when he obtained the series of 30 Visions of the Aires or Athyrs, in accordance with the System partially worked out by Dr. Dee and Sir Edward Kelly. Some of these visions are very wonderful indeed, and I cannot refrain from quoting a part of his Magical Record on the subject. The following is chosen because it introduces the Angel Madimi, the same who first appeared to Dr. Dee.

*The Cry Of The 17th Aethyr
Which Is Called Tan.*

"Into the stone there first cometh the head of a dragon, and then the Angel Madimi. She is not the mere elemental that one would suppose from the account of Casaubon. I enquire why her form is different.

She says: Since all things are God, in all things thou seest just so much of God as thy capacity affordeth thee. But behold! Thou must pierce deeply into this Aethyr before true images appear. For TAN is that which transformeth judgment into justice. BAL is the sword, and TAN the balances.

A pair of balances appears in the stone, and on the bar of the balance is written: Motion about a point is iniquity.

And behind the balances is a plume, luminous, azure. And somehow connected with the plume, but I cannot divine how, are the words: Breath is iniquity. (That is, any wind must stir the feather of truth.)

And behind the plume is a shining filament of quartz, suspended vertically from the abyss to the abyss. And in the midst is a winged disk of some extremely delicate, translucent substance, on which is written in the "dagger" alphabet: Torsion is iniquity. (This means, that Rashith Ha-Gilgalim is the first appearance of evil.)

And now an Angel appears, like as he were carven in black diamonds. And he cries: Woe unto the Second, whom all nations of men call the First. Woe unto the First, whom all grades of Adepts call the First. Woe unto me, for I, even as they, have worshipped him. But she whose paps are the galaxies, and he that never shall be known, in them is no motion. For the Infinite Without filleth all and moveth not, and the Infinite Within goeth indeed; but it is no odds, else were the space-marks confounded.

And now the Angel is but a shining speck of blackness in the midst of a tremendous sphere of liquid and vibrating light, at first gold, then becoming green, and lastly pure gold. And I see that the green of Libra is made up of the yellow of air and the blue of water, swords and cups, judgment and mercy. And this word TAN meaneth mercy. And the feather of Maat is blue because the truth of justice is mercy. And a voice cometh, as it were the music of the ripples of the surface of the sphere: Truth is delight. (This means that the Truth of the universe is delight.)

Another voice cometh; it is the voice of a mighty Angel, all in silver; the scales of his armour and the plumes of his wings are like mother-of-pearl in a framework of silver. And he sayeth: Justice is the equity that ye have made for yourselves between truth and falsehood. But in Truth there is nothing of this, for there is only Truth. Your falsehood is but a little falser than your truth. Yet by your truth shall ye come to Truth. Your truth is your troth with Adonai the Beloved one. And the Chymical Marriage of the Alchemists beginneth with a Weighing, and he that is not found wanting hath within him one spark of fire, so dense and so intense that it cannot be moved, though all the winds of heaven should clamour against it, and all the waters of the abyss surge upon it to smother it. Nay, it shall not be moved.

And this is the fire of which it is written: "Hear thou the voice of fire!" And the voice of Afire is the second chapter of the Book of the Law, that is revealed unto him that is a score and half a score and three that are scores, and six, by Aiwass, that is his guardian, the mighty Angel that extendeth from the first unto the last, and maketh known the mysteries that are beyond. And the method and the form of invocation whereby a man shall attain to the knowledge and conversation of his Holy Guardian Angel shall be given unto thee in the proper place, and seeing that the word is deadlier than lightning, do thou meditate straightly thereupon, solitary, in a place where is no living thing visible, but only the light of the sun. And thy head shall be bare. Thus mayest thou become fitted to receive this, the holiest of the Mysteries. And it is the holiest of the Mysteries because it is the Next Step. And those Mysteries which lie beyond, though they be holier, are not holy unto thee, but only remote. (The sense of this passage seems to be, that the holiness of a thing implies its personal relation with one, just as one cannot blaspheme an unknown god, because one does not know what to say to annoy him. And this explains the perfect inefficiency of those who try to insult the saints; the most violent attacks are very often merely clumsy compliments.)

Now the Angel is spread completely over the Globe, a dewy film of silver upon that luminous blue.

And a great voice cries: Behold the Queen of Heaven, how she hath woven her robes from the loom of justice. For as that straight path of the Arrow cleaving the Rainbow became righteousness in her that sitteth in the hall of double truth, so at last is she exalted unto the throne of the High Priestess, the Priestess of the Silver Star, wherein also is thine Angel made manifest

And this is the mystery of the camel that is ten days in the desert, and is not athirst, because he hath within him that water which is the dew distilled from the Night of Nuit. Triple is the cord of silver, that it may not be loosed; and three score and a half a score and three is the number of the name of my name, for that the ineffable wisdom, that also is of the sphere of the stars, informeth me. Thus am I crowned with the triangle that is about the eye, and therefore is my number three. And in me there is no imperfection, because through me descendeth the influence of TARO. And that is also the number of Aiwass the mighty Angel, the Minister of Silence.

And even as the shew-stone burneth thy forehead with its intolerable flame, so he who hath known me, though but from afar, is marked out and chosen from among men, and he shall never turn back or turn aside, for he hath made the link that is not to be broken, nay, not by the malice of the Four Great Princes of the evil of the world, nor by Choronzon, that mighty Devil, nor by the wrath of God, nor by affliction and feebleness of the soul.

Yet with this assurance be not thou content; for though thou hast wings of the Eagle, they are vain, except they be joined to the shoulders of the Bull. Now, therefore, I send forth a shaft of my light, even as a ladder let down from the heaven upon the earth, and by this black cross of Themis that I hold before thine eyes, do I swear unto thee that the path shall be open henceforth for evermore.

There is a clash of a myriad silver cymbals, and silence. And then three times a note is struck upon a bell, which sounds like my holy Tibetan bell, that is made of electrum magicum.

I am happily returned unto the earth. Bou-Saada.

December 2, 1909. 12:15-2 A. M.

The above example of one of the most perfect types of Symbolic Visions cannot be fully appreciated by those who are unacquainted with

CRYSTAL GAZING

the true Keys of the Holy Qabalah, and with some of the Mysteries of the New Aeon. Those who have made some study of "Q. B. L.", of the "Tree of Life", the Tarot, etc., will soon discover a great many underlying meanings, and to them the perfect consistency of all the symbolism, will be quite apparent. In any case, even those who have little knowledge of such matters, will recognize the beauty, sublimity, and greatness of this type of Vision, compared with any of a more partial nature. Of course, this is but one of a series, and by itself is not very explanatory, but I may add, that all these Visions were of a definitely Initiatory nature – so far as the Seer was concerned – and at the same time they have a perfectly true Universal Application. It is a pity this cannot be said in regard to the average "crystal reading". But the concentration of mind obtained by the earnest student of crystal-gazing, may, as before remarked, result in visions of a much more important character, if the seer is sufficiently interested in Truth to learn to make his own Inner Vision, Crystal Clear.

VII

Of The Ultimate Crystal

"In the sphere I am everywhere the centre, as she, the circumference, is nowhere found." – Liber Legis. Ch. II Verse 3.

WE are now nearing the end of our journey in search of the True Crystal. Before, however, we treat of the ultimate conceptions, we should devote a little more time to matters less transcendent in their nature.

This little treatise, while giving as wide a view as possible of the whole subject, aims to be intensely practical and helpful to all who may read it. Some will be at one stage of development, others will have reached a different level, but the author trusts that all will obtain some hints that may actually be put into practice, and thus lead the seeker to a clearer and better *understanding of* himself and others.

Here are a few practical hints: A diet of fruit and vegetables may have its advantages by making the student more susceptible to visions of a clairvoyant type. On the other hand a mixed diet suits some people far better, and may give more real staying power. Don't become a "diet crank" you will have no time for anything else more important. Use your common sense – experiment if you like – but don't form habits. The best type of man or woman is the one who can eat anything, and does eat anything according to the natural promptings of his or her being, and that without causing digestive troubles.

Don't do any practice after a full meal, or when very tired; this would not be giving Nature a proper chance, and your practice must suffer accordingly.

Rather be the tortoise than the hare. Real progress is made despite obstacles, and the more obstacles we meet - and overcome - the stronger becomes our will.

You are practically *bound to obtain* what you *truly ask for*. Be sure of what you really want before you ask for it.

Take plenty of fresh air and exercise, and don't become so obsessed with dark seances that you overlook the value of Sunlight.

Your first duty to Humanity is self-improvement. Man is ignorant of the nature and powers of his own being. Until he has obtained a scientific knowledge of himself, he cannot really expect to aid others.

It requires much more study and effort to Know Yourself, than it does to give others advice they do not need. Learn to mind your own business, and in time others will follow your example.

CRYSTAL GAZING

Learn to speak the truth, and you will begin to notice when you are telling lies.

Remember that even truth is relative. There is but one Truth and that lies at the End of the Path. Yet seek Truth, and be content with nothing less. We live in a world of appearances. There seem to be innumerable, "Pairs of Opposites" till the final Pair has been realized and Mated. Then we shall "See things as they are."

In the meanwhile there are many stages, each nearer to the Truth, wherein we shall still see things only as they APPEAR. All Visions, however high, fall under this heading.

The Highest States of Consciousness are FORMLESS, and the final State is of Crystalline Purity. There is, however, "That which remains" viz: perfect Bliss.

A short description might well be given of "Visions" of an intermediate type, such as we term Astral Visions, as this may be of interest to students who have traveled some distance on the path, but who, as yet, have not realized results such as we described in the last Chapter.

The following is from the Author's Occult Record while a Neophyte of the Great Order. It is of the type called an Astral Journey, when the Seer actually "travels" in his "Body of Light."

FRATER ACHAD

"Nov. 28, 1913. 11:5 to 11:27 P. M. Drew, with wand, in front of me, a circle (three times round) and formed astral in that. Rose to a great height. Suddenly, as it were, a rope flashed round me and fell, forming a spiral, ever widening, at the top of which I sat. Stood up on this, only to fall, down, down, down, not quite vertically, into the water. Rising again, and striking out, I, after a short while perceived a boat, something like a gondola, and swam towards it. It was rowed by a dark-skinned man, old and wrinkled, whom I at first thought to be an Indian. As I reached the boat and put my hand on the side, it seemed as if he would strike at me with his oar, but no, he grinned, and I drew myself into the boat and sat in the forepart, which was high and covered with a sort of hood. Presently, it struck me that the man was not living but dead (Death). We then drifted in a mist, and all became blank for awhile; the memory of boat, man and self, were all but lost.

When the mist cleared I realized that the man was no longer there, and I myself guided the boat. Coming back out of the mist the waters were blue and no longer black, and I realized, that day was breaking. Gradually I watched the Sunrise, and set the boat in that direction, rowing so as to keep my face to the Sun. It seemed like a Portal; but, keeping on, it presently rose, and by the time it was getting high

CRYSTAL GAZING

in the heavens I perceived a fair city ahead. Domes, Minarets, etc. Arriving there, I for the first time noticed I was dark skinned and clad in a loincloth. Landing, I was surrounded by men in an Eastern costume, Arabs or Turks, I thought them.

One old man took me by the hand, I made the sign of the Pentagram over him, but he smiled and said "Come along, it's all right," and led me along a street paved with cobbles, the houses of which overhung, till we reached a sort of mosque.

Entering this, he led me to the altar, which was supported by brackets from the wall, and above which was a beautiful stained window. At the sides were thin columns and sort of boxes, similar to theatre boxes. We knelt at the altar; and he took my hand and said: "Raise your consciousness." I perceived a star and crescent above me, and a cross dimly formulated in the background.

After this, the astral seemed to coincide with the body: but consciousness of the astral surroundings was still clear. Continued to raise consciousness, and to send out thoughts of Love. Perceived around me innumerable streams of thought, interlacing and like a net-work, and when the Love-thought was sent out, the whole net sparkled, as with little specks of gold. Continued in this thought for some minutes, and, gradually returned to normal. Gave thanks and entered diary."

I quote this Vision, chiefly because it was not what it should have been, and because this gives me the opportunity of adding the Comments made upon it by my Guru. He wrote:

"Very nearly in serious trouble, my young and rash friend! It seems that you must go up well outside earth-attraction if you wish to get good astrals. It sounds Sunday-school talk, and I can give no reason. But I've tried repeatedly going horizontally and downwards, always with the same result. Gross and hostile things are below, pure being above. The vision is good enough for what it is; it is clear and coherent. But I see no trace of scientific method in directing the vision. I explain further in the general comment. O. M."

Such advice is worthy of the notice of every "seer" for much of it applies to other forms of work. To search the earth plane by means of visions, is practically valueless, and often positively harmful. We can travel to another city for a few dollars without expenditure of valuable occult power, but we have a right to use it to examine "Things above" which cannot be reached by means of a material aeroplane. We should always make use of physical means on the physical plane if possible, people make the greatest mistakes

CRYSTAL GAZING

by "mixing the planes." That is the chief trouble with "mental science" "mental healing" and what not. We must learn to adjust things on their own planes. The Physical by Physical, the Astral by Astral, the Mental by Mental, and The Spiritual by Spiritual methods. When we have straightened out these different levels of consciousness, a certain harmony will be apparent on all planes, which in the end results in perfect Unity. The Method of trying to control ideas of one plane, by means of those of another, is a wrong one. Remember things are always true on their own plane, but in very few instances are they true on another. That is why we should examine our visions scientifically, while they are present in our consciousness, but when that consciousness becomes aware of the material plane once more, we should place little, if any reliance, on the truth of our vision, as corresponding to events of everyday life.

I may perhaps quote one more vision, of a slightly higher type, since it was invoked by means of Will and by scientific methods. Visions are of little real value unless WILLED.

This time the vision was undertaken in order to discover the answer to a definite Examination Question set by the Order.

"Invoke Mercury and Hod, and travel till you meet the Unicorn mentioned in Liber

FRATER ACHAD

LXV, Chapter III, verse 2. Report its conversation fully."

This is the kind of question you must fit yourselves to answer. Something you could not possibly obtain by other means. Few people realize that on the Astral Plane are the Records from which such Inspired and Holy Books as Liber LXV are written, and that these Records may again be Invoked by proper means.

"March 24th, 1914. 9:40 to 10:50 P. M. During the day I prepared a Circle of Orange, about 5 ft. in diameter (the largest I could make in the little room I am using) and within it, an eight-pointed star of yellow. Within that again an Octagon. A Red upright Tau in the centre, and eight small red pentagrams at the points of the star to represent lights; for there was no room to use them with safety. The whole was very crude, but the best I could do with the materials at hand.

Having robed and entered the temple, I made a general Invocation (impromptu) of the Lord of the Universe, and traced the circle and figures with the wand. Performed the Lesser Banishing Ritual of the Pentagram; then Invoked "Water" and sprinkled the circle to purify it. Performed the Lesser Ritual of the Hexagon, followed by Invocation of Mercury and

Hod, (impromptu) with appropriate Hexagram.

Lit incense. Made a further statement of my intention. Knelt in the centre of Circle and tried to formulate a "White Astral" with no very great success at first. Afterwards, I forgot about the material body and began to get some result.

Found my "astral" floating upon a dark sea on a sort of plank. The moon was shining above, and the thought came to me that 'perhaps the Moon represented the Unicorn I had set out to seek', but I decided it was not so.

Rising higher, I tried to identify myself with the moon, and then turned and faced the Sun; looking along the Ray as a Path. I had the impression of being a little child.

About this time I was reminded of my physical body by a pressure on the brain, head and neck; a sort of frozen rigidity, which caused me to lose concentration on the astral for a little while. I determined to keep on, however, and astrally performed the Lesser Banishing Ritual of the Pentagram. When I came to the words: "In the column stands the Six-Rayed Star" I seemed to rise quite easily.

Traveled about, with no particular visions, seeking the Unicorn. I obtained an idea of a unicorn, but not very distinctly, and spoke to it. It informed me that it had no desire to converse. I made the sign of the Pentagram over it, whereupon, it said that it was not that which I sought. This being my own opinion also, I left it, and rose higher to try again.

This time I got a clearer idea of the Unicorn, and began to converse with it.

We were on the edge of a wood, beneath a night sky. It told me to look up, and having done so, I perceived a comet flash across the sky and disappear. Turning back, I questioned him, and he answered; 'All men are thus, the Universe is thus'. So I gathered from his words that a fragment appears for a moment (or a period) and disappears, leaving no trace.

I felt that this was something I must get to understand, when he said: 'Look again' and this time a meteor flashed and then struck the earth. And he said: 'Sometimes it is thus, and there appears to be pain as a result'. Then I said to him: 'Do I understand that man appears for a moment only, and is forever gone again?' And he answered 'The comet remains travelling in its ellipse, and only disappears from sight. Further, he told me to look again, and I beheld a fixed star, shining in the blue. Turning again to him, I asked what this meant; and he answered: 'The Masters are thus, they travel no more, but give Light'. Then I asked if I should attain to this, to which he replied 'Yea, but not yet. Thou must be as a comet

CRYSTAL GAZING

until after a while thou strikest, a star, and becoming one with it, remain fixed.'

And I understood that there was nothing further to be said at that time. So I returned, and having given thanks, entered these experiences in my diary."

There is not much further to be said, so far as this little book is concerned, though there is much that might, and will be said at the proper time. The early vision, above recorded, took place 8 years ago, and much has transpired since then.

It may be remarked that this vision had a far wider and deeper application than ever the Seer realized at the time, part of this became more apparent many years later, there is still much to be accomplished.

But let me call your attention to the Star. It is written, in Liber Legis, The Book of the Law, "Every man and every woman is a star." What does this mean? It would take another and longer treatise, to tell you. This much may be said, however:

At the CENTRE of our Being is the Star of Unconquered Will, that is the True or Divine Will, the Will of the Universe. Each must discover this Star in his own being, and putting his personal will in line with Its Guidance, become an active and conscious cooperator in the Universal Plan. This Star is of Intense brilliance. It is the Diamond Soul, the only

Veil about the Innermost Essential Self. It is thus the ULTIMATE CRYSTAL, of which it is written by Our Lady Nuit – Goddess of the Starry Heavens – Who represents INFINITE SPACE or the Universal Crystalline Sphere:

"Worship then the Khabs (Star) and behold my light shed over you!"

When we have discovered this Central Light of our Being, and learned to Concentrate the Mind thereon, we shall begin the Ultimate Practice of Crystal Gazing.

We shall find the Star Rays from the Universal Sphere centered in us, and when the focus becomes perfect, shall discover, that this CENTRE is everywhere and the circumference nowhere. Then all our conceptions of Crystalline Spheres will melt into That which is Without Limit:

Perfect Crystalline Vision.

FIN.

AFTERWARDS:

AN EXCERPT FROM
THE EQUINOX, Vol. III, No. I
LIBER CLXV:
'A Master of the Temple'
by The Master Therion

CHARLES STANSFELD JONES, whom I usually mention by the motto V.I.O., which he took on becoming a Probationer of the A∴A∴,* made his entry into this World by the usual and approved method, on April 2nd, 1886 E. V., having only escaped becoming an April Fool by delaying a day to summon up enough courage to turn out once more into this cold and uninviting World. Having been oiled, smacked and allowed to live, we shall trouble no further about the details of his career until 1906, when, having reached the age of 20 years, he began to turn his attention toward the Mysteries, and to investigate Spiritualism, chiefly with the idea of dis-proving it. From this year his interest in the Occult seems to date, and it was about this time that he first consciously aspired to find, and get

---

* [Charles Stansfeld Jones (1886-1950) later took the motto "Achad" upon his elevation to the A∴A∴ grade of Neophyte. – Eds.]

into touch with, a True Occult Order. This aspiration was fulfilled three years later, when he had an opportunity to become a Probationer of the A∴ A∴, and immediately grasped it; but during those three years his researches led him into varied paths: Spiritualism, Faithism and other Isms on the one hand, and "The Europe," "The Leicester," and "The Cosy Corner" on the other: last, but not least, into Marriage, a difficult thing to put on one side and perhaps best left on the other. Having then plunged wholeheartedly into this final experiment, becoming as it were *"Omnia in Uno"* for a time, he emerged in a frame of mind well suited to the study of Scientific Illuminism, of which he was much in need, and, having signed the Probationer's Pledge Form on December 24th, 1909, E.V., he took — after careful thought — the Motto *"Unus in Omnibus"* and has been riding very comfortably ever since.

THE MASTER THERION
London, 1919

Jabberwoke Pocket Occult Collection

CRYSTAL GAZING by Frater Achad

Thus, it is hoped, all will be satisfied; and should the satisfaction be equal to that of the Author at the opportunity to herald the Light – however faintly – the Ultimate Crystalline Sphere.

ISBN: 978-1-954873-36-0
$11.00 USD
FraterAchadCrystalGazing.com

HEAVENLY BRIDEGROOMS by Ida Craddock

"One of the most remarkable human documents ever produced... This book is of incalculable value to every student of Occult matters. No Magick library is complete without it" – A.C.

ISBN: 978-1-954873-21-6
$14.00 USD
HeavenlyBridegrooms.com

MOONCHILD by Aleister Crowley

The cattiest & messiest novel from the transcriber of the Wickedest Man in England. Hiding behind the guise of fiction, Moonchild is the Beast's platform to slander his many nemeses inside the spiritualist circles of London.

ISBN: 978-1-954873-53-7
$19.00 USD /
AleisterCrowleyMoonchild.com

THE KYBALION by Three Initiates

There is no portion of the occult teachings which has been so closely guarded as the fragments of the Hermetic Teachings, the Great Central Sun of Occultism, whose rays have illuminated the teachings promulgated since time.

ISBN: 978-1-954873-08-7
$14.00 USD
ThreeInitiatesKybalion.com

THE SO-CALLED OCCULT by Carl Jung

A 20-year-old Carl Jung attends his cousin's seance leading to a psychological investigation of haunting witch-sleeps, and delicious bliss that unravels in obsession.

ISBN: 978-1-954873-39-1
$14.00 USD
TheSoCalledOccult.com

THE GREAT GOD PAN *by Arthur Machen*

A classic of pagan horror that follows the trail of destruction left in the wake of a mysterious socialite, as she serves the will of her shadowy, horned benefactor.

ISBN: 978-1-954873-35-3
$14.00 USD
AllHailPan.com

THE WITCH CULT *by Margaret Murray*

Firsthand accounts of a pre-Christian witch cult that worshiped the Horned God of fertility—whose Christian persecutors referred to him as the Devil—and the nocturnal rites performed at the witches' Sabbath.

ISBN: 978-1-954873-33-9
$19.00 USD
TheWitchCult.com

THE BOOK OF LIES *by Frater Perdurabo*

A collection of falsehoods from Dionysus, received by the mysterious Frater Perdurabo and the Scarlet Woman LAYLAH. This wicked book is said to contain within its pages the secret truth of the universe . . . readers beware.

ISBN: 978-1-954873-37-7
$14.00 USD
FaleslyCalledBreaks.com

A MIDSOMMAR NIGHT'S DREAM *by William Shakespeare*

The timeless ethereal tale of four Lovers who wander too close to the games of Titania and Oberon, the Faerie Queen and King, and their encounters with the archetypal Tickster Puck and all the fantastical beings whom inhabit the woodland realm.

ISBN: 978-1-954873-54-4
$11.00 USD
MidsommarNightsDream.com

SATAN: A NOVEL *by Mark Twain*

The greatest and final novel from the master of American fiction, Mark Twain's fable of an angelic visitation in the Austrian countryside reveals the solipsism of its author, and his belief of the unreality of our collective dream.

ISBN: 978-1-954873-59-9
$16.00 USD
MarkTwainSatan.com

JABBERWOKE © MMXXI

Wholesale Inquiries:
contact@jabberwokebooks.com

www.ingramcontent.com/pod-product-compliance
Lightning Source LLC
Chambersburg PA
CBHW021448070526
44577CB00002B/304